SHELF WORK IN LIBRARIES

SHELF
WORK

IN LIBRARIES

by William H. Jesse
Director of Libraries
The University of Tennessee
Knoxville

Chicago

AMERICAN LIBRARY ASSOCIATION

1952

PREFACE

The author's intention has been to cover the entire area of shelf work in all types of libraries and to include material both practical and theoretical which would be of interest and value to all librarians, school, public, college and university, or special. The contents are aimed specifically at the supervisor of shelf work who wants to know what should be done, why, and how it may best be accomplished. While the intention of this book can be stated this simply, the author hardly presumes to think that the tortuous course between the theoretical and the practical has been maneuvered with complete success.

Grateful acknowledgement is made to those librarians who read the manuscript and offered many helpful suggestions, comments, and criticisms: Dr. Edward A. Wight, Professor of Librarianship, University of California, Berkeley, formerly Assistant Director, Newark Public Library; Mrs. Ruth Williams Mitchell, formerly Head of Circulation, Lawson McGhee Public Library, Knoxville; Miss Georgia G. McAfee, retired, formerly Librarian, Lima, Ohio, Public Library; Miss Priscilla Lantz, Associate Professor of Library Service, University of Tennessee, formerly Librarian of the South Junior High School, Quincy; Mrs. Evalyn Willey Miles, Assistant, University of Illinois Library School, formerly of the Manual High School Library, Louisville; Miss Agnes Gregory, Assistant Professor, School of Library Training and Service, Florida State University; Mr. Wayne S. Yenawine, Head of the Circulation Department, University of Illinois Library; and Mr. Arnold H. Trotier, Assistant Director for Technical Departments, University of Illinois Library. Many suggestions regarding scope, approach, and treatment were made by Mrs. Pauline J. Love, Chief, Publishing Department, American Library Association, and by Mr. Everett O. Fontaine, former Chief. Much help was received from members of the University of Tennessee Library staff; particular thanks are due Mr. William M. Robarts, for gathering the material for Chapters 4 and 5, and Miss Katherine Montague, for assistance in checking the manuscript with Miss Daphne Harris, who typed the manuscript.

William H. Jesse
Knoxville
January 22, 1952

CONTENTS

SHELF WORK IN LIBRARIES

SHELF-WORK IN LIBRARIES

Chapter 1

SHELF WORK--OBJECTIVES,

ORGANIZATION, AND PRACTICE

Objectives of shelf work

The objectives of shelf work like the over-all objectives
of the library are to give adequate and efficient service to
the library user. More specifically, the shelf worker is
primarily concerned with delivering a book when it is
wanted, returning it to its assigned place when it is no
longer needed, and seeing that it is properly cared for until
it is wanted again. The concern of the shelf-work supervisor, whether in the large or small library, is naturally
much broader. He is responsible for, or shares decisions
concerning, the arrangement of the collection so as to bring
the most used books near service points without too much
disregard of the classification scheme; the special shelving
of oversized books; housing and arrangement of nonbook
materials; the exploitation of architectural and esthetic
possibilities of building areas in which readers are in direct contact with books; order and cleanliness within his
area; and the training and supervision of his staff. He also
has such other duties as planning and executing of major
shifts or moving of the book collection and inventory with
its follow-up.

Organization of shelf work

Shelf work in small and medium-sized libraries is normally assigned to the circulation department. It is done by
the personnel who serve at the circulation desk or by one or
more shelf workers who are a part of the circulation staff.
The two principal reasons for this are: (1) good administrative practice requires that this part-time work be done
by someone doing related work, or that no separate administrative unit be set up for such a small staff, as the case

1

applies; (2) since those who shelve the books are in most cases the same assistants who page the books, and since paging[1] is an integral part of circulation, the assistants doing shelf work logically belong in the circulation department.

In the large library which houses most of its collection in the stacks of the main building and has most of its circulation directly from these stacks, shelf work might best be organized under a single administrative head. This shelf-work supervisor should be immediately responsible to the most logical superior officer: the head of circulation, the readers' division chief, the assistant librarian, or the librarian, depending upon the over-all administrative organization of the library.

In the large library which places most of its books on shelves to which the public has direct access or which has its greatest circulation from service points such as reading rooms or branches, shelf work should for the most part be the responsibility of the staff members at these service points. The various systems have long been established and fully and formally described and weighed.[2] Large public libraries have for many years assigned stack space to both the reference and circulation departments.[3] While it might be advantageous to have a single person responsible for shelf work throughout the library, this work may be assigned to various departments and still be correlated by a single staff member.

The universality of shelf work makes it a natural and relatively simple area of work in which a certain amount of consistency can be attained, even if the responsibility cannot be vested centrally. The more rapidly a collection is growing the more desirable it becomes to consider possible advantages of centralizing shelving responsibility, for growth creates and intensifies problems of shelf work.

[1]Note: "Paging" has various meanings in different library systems. In this book "paging" means "to fetch a book."

[2]Seymour Robb, "Library Step-Children--the Bookstacks," Library Journal, LXII (1937), 273-76.

[3]American Library Association, A Survey of Libraries in the United States, Vol. II, Service to Readers in Public Libraries and in College and University Libraries (Chicago: American Library Association, 1926), p. 91.

2 Shelf work

Arrangement of the book collection

The arrangement of the books on the shelves is important in making books readily accessible to the reader and
the staff. Theoretically, at least, there are two basic as-
sumptions regarding the arrangement of the book collection: (1) each book has its permanent location in some particular spot on some particular shelf; or (2) each book has
a location relative to the rest of the books in the collection
according to its classification. In most libraries in the
United States, books are placed in a sequence based on
classification; only occasionally is the principle of fixed
location followed.

Shelf order may be varied (1) to modify an existing
classification scheme as in the case of pulling all the books
on all aspects of technology out of their several logical
places in the classification order and putting them into a
technology collection; or (2) to serve as a temporary reclassification device as when certain books are drawn out
of their class order and put temporarily on open shelves.

Collections most commonly shelved separately are fiction, mystery stories, westerns, biographies, reference
books, new books, reserved books, most useful books, most
popular books, most used books, and "best" books. In addition, there are subject approach sections, such as business,
science, history, local history, and international relations.
The number and nature of these special collections are
limited only by the imagination, energy, skill, and ability of
the librarian. In deciding what should be done about special
arrangements of material, the librarian should take into
account the quality and size of the book collection, the way
in which the books have been processed, the layout of the
building, and the equipment and its arrangement for shelving the separate collections. Good shelf work can never be
accomplished if all these factors are not recognized.

While shelf order may be varied, frequent abuses of
this practice are found. The principal abuse is the care-
less and unsound but sometimes unavoidable practice of
shelving books in so many different ways in response to
immediate service demands that need for reclassification
may be indicated. Since reclassification is not to be considered lightly, some compromise between class number
order and practical order should be made. Certainly,

3

services outrank order and system in most modern libraries, but good service depends largely upon good order and system. It is possible to go too far in shelving books out of regular order and in extensive reclassification. It is also possible to go too far in substituting circulation charges for catalog location stamps. These problems can be met intelligently only when considered jointly, whether by the collective professional judgment of a group of specialists on a large library staff or the single, but conceivably just as professional, judgment of the librarian in a one-man library.

Shelf arrangement can go far toward solving problems created by classification, but it should never be depended upon to do the whole job. It will be observed that often where arrangement is expected to solve classification problems, shelf work will break down, with the result that only the veteran staff member or constant user will know where to find the books. Training new assistants, especially pages (where turnover is usually high), becomes an expensive and depressing process.

Shelving practice

Open shelves and stacks. Present day trends, reflected in the planning of many new large libraries, indicate that a much higher percentage of the books will not be in isolated bookstacks, but will be made available to readers on an informal basis. As the trend develops, shelf-work practices in the large university library and in the small public library will become more similar. In the future, university libraries will be concerned more and more with the matter of administering the book collections from open shelves (shelves to which readers have direct access for the examination of books), heretofore a problem more typical of the public, school, and college library. The great increase in the amount of shelf work which follows these educational-architectural decisions will be more than justified by the increased accessibility of the books to the reader. But such trends in library architecture are slow in emerging as patterns because buildings are by their nature not subject to rapid and fundamental change. Consequently, most librarians who work with collections of substantial size still have typical stack areas for housing most of their books.

There will always be, and probably always should be, the great storehouses of infrequently consulted books which are best shelved in stacks. The indiscriminate inter-shelving of some of the most used books along with some of the least used books is being attacked, not only because of the difficulty of getting the most needed book and the reader together, but also because the little used book should be removed from its expensive and strategic location in the main library and relegated to semi-storage in less com-petitive and less expensive building space.[4]

Fiction. In most small and medium-sized public li-braries fiction is shelved separately, usually in an open-shelf collection. Ordinarily books are arranged in alpha-betical order according to the authors' last names. From this point on, practice varies; several titles by a particular author may or may not be arranged alphabetically or books by authors with the same surname may be grouped to-gether. The shelving time saved by this last arrangement may be more than lost in readers' and staff time when there is need to locate a specific title.

Fiction can be and often is shelved by type, such as de-tective and mystery stories, western stories, romances, and short stories. It can of course be treated as literature. While some libraries do classify all fiction as literature most do so only with collected works of standard novelists, translations, collections of short stories, and similar cate-gories. Students in school libraries usually like to have fiction grouped by type, as mystery, western etc. This is often done in special displays, but attempting to maintain more permanent type divisions poses a constant problem where shelving is usually done by a large number of student assistants. Since such shelving practices also tend to en-courage people to read more narrowly they are not usually followed in school libraries. Short story collections, how-

---

[4]Ralph E. Ellsworth and Norman L. Kilpatrick, "Midwest Reaches for the Stars," College and Research Libraries, IX (1948), 136; Keyes D. Metcalf, "The New England Deposit Library," Library Quarterly, XII (1942), 622-28; Leroy Charles Merritt, "The Book Stock," in Herman H. Fussler (ed.), Library Build-ings for Library Service (Chicago: American Library Association, 1947) p.56-70; Fremont Rider, Compact Book Storage, Some Suggestions toward a New Method-ology for the Shelving of Less Used Research Materials (New York: The Hadham Press, 1949); "Plans Completed for the Midwest Inter-Library Center Building," College and Research Libraries, XI (1950), 264.

ever, are usually shelved separately, not as literature but as a special section of fiction.

Nonfiction. Books of nonfiction are customarily arranged by call numbers with volumes in sets being kept in numerical order. Shelving of entire classes or subclasses apart from the rest of the classed-order collection presents fewer shelving problems than pulling out only certain titles. However, the latter practice usually results in a better special collection as far as the reader is concerned.

New books. Many libraries shelve recent fiction by itself, making a special collection within a special collection. New nonfiction titles, too, are usually separated from the older ones and placed on open shelves or display tables in prominent locations. The disadvantages of segregating new titles would seem to be more than offset by the fact that so many readers want immediate and easy access to the new books as such; that is, they want to read a new book because it is new.

While the practice of segregating new books is often followed in university and large municipal reference libraries, it is not nearly so important as in the small and medium-sized public library; for in the research libraries the reader is more apt to want a particular title, and the fact that a book is new is of less importance to him. However, even the research library, especially one also serving undergraduates, will ordinarily call attention to its new acquisitions by separate shelving at some public point. In this case some of the most interesting titles among the new acquisitions will not be new books at all. As a matter of fact, in many subject fields the older the title the more interesting it would seem to be to certain subject specialists. While "new books" is a very loose description of such a section of new acquisitions, the fundamental idea is the same as in the small or medium-sized public library--to call attention to and make readily available the books which are new to a library. School libraries, except for special displays of new acquisitions, do not usually shelve new books by themselves, since this tends to overemphasize the new. Many students tend to confine their attention to the new too much as it is, especially with fiction, and would see less of the better older titles unless they were all shelved together.

The individual or the department responsible for shelving this material will want to be sure that there exists some record of this temporary location of these new books; for it is the business of shelf work to make sure that all books belonging to the library are either in their proper places or are accounted for (except those which have been loaned, the records for which are the property of circulation or other lending departments). The best device for recording a temporary location is a charge in the circulation file. If the library does not have a circulation file arranged by classification order (and many libraries do not maintain such a record), there are several other devices which have been tried with some success.

One such device is to keep a constantly revised typescript of the new books, usually arranged by author's surname. Additions can be made to this typescript, if double-spaced, by penciling in the title added, and deletions can be made by crossing out a line. Before a new typescript is made, it is well to check the new book shelf for titles which are missing, or which have not circulated, or which have been on the new book shelf beyond a point allowing them to be considered new. The same kind of list can be placed on the end of the range or bookcase which contains the new books. In some libraries the new book list is made up in multiple copies, and corrections and changes made systematically for the group. Only the arrangement of a particular library and the amount and kind of service that goes on in it can determine whether or not multiple copies are worth the additional effort. This changing list of new books can also be kept on cards.

In order that the new book may be returned to its proper temporary location, it may be equipped with a gummed label or carry a temporary location stamp or symbol on the date-due slip or the charge card or the charge card pocket (according to the circulation charging system used in the particular library).

Block arrangement. Block arrangement is the method of shelving books in regular shelf-to-shelf, case-to-case order according to classification. An interesting variation is accomplished by placing an occasional section of non-fiction in the congested fiction areas. This variation is designed quite practically to relieve the crowding that often exists when all the fiction is shelved closely together in a busy public library.

Ribbon arrangement. Ribbon arrangement, which was on a definite decline when the American Library Association Survey was made,[5] seems to be increasingly less popular, except perhaps in the case of some school libraries and children's rooms in public libraries. While this arrangement varies somewhat in its actual operation, it consists primarily of placing nonfiction on the upper and lower shelves and fiction on the middle ones. Historically, at least, this arrangement was supposed to increase the reading of nonfiction by a kind of enforced browsing on the part of avid readers of fiction, and there is some reason to believe that the reading of nonfiction does get some stimulation from this source. Ribbon arrangement does help relieve crowding at the fiction shelves.

Oversize volumes. Oversize volumes must be shelved in a manner which will not interfere with the most economical arrangement of the smaller volumes. The problems are old. Efforts to solve them have at times gone to such lengths as providing for the shelving of volumes on the basis of size, beginning with the largest books on the bottom shelf and, gradually tapering in size, the smallest on the top shelf. This, of course, prevents adequate subject arrangement. With the adoption of subject classification schemes, such as the Dewey Decimal System, a size mark was added to the oversize book's call number, and these volumes were placed on the bottom shelves throughout the stack area or in a separate shelving sequence on each floor level.[6] For further discussion of this subject with respect to the large library, see Shelving for Oversize Books, Chapter IV.

Large libraries are not the only ones that have to deal with oversize books. In the school library, especially elementary, they present a real problem in shelving. Books for small children are separated from others partly for the convenience of younger readers, but also because of special shelf requirements for picture books. One of the best methods for shelving these special materials employs vertical panels (at intervals of about 6 inches) on each shelf in the section. Modern trends in the format of informational books for older children (as pictorial geog-

[5] American Library Association, op. cit., p.27.
[6] Frank Carney, "Some Problems of a Shelf Department," Library Journal, XXXIII (1908), 433-37.

raphies and histories) are increasing this problem of shelving oversize books.

Bound periodicals. Bound periodicals can be removed entirely from their classified order and placed in a separate area, though supervision and circulation may remain a duty of the circulation department. Many public libraries find the practice of placing entire dependence for location upon an alphabetical-by-title arrangement quite satisfactory.

Rare books. The few suggestions offered here concerning rare books are limited, first, to shelf work only and, second, to the small library with only a few (or at most only a few hundred) rare books. The larger rare book collections will need, and will probably have, a rare-books specialist on the staff to whom these necessarily limited suggestions will appear elementary. Do not mark on or in the book itself with ink; use pencil, use it lightly, and use it sparingly. Do not perforate. Do not stamp. Do not emboss. If a call number is necessary, paste a label on the side of the book (not the spine) and write the call number on the label. Do not allow readers to use ink in taking notes. Put the book in a box or extra covers if it has to be housed in a dusty or dirty atmosphere or where there is too much sunshine directly upon it. House in locked, dirt-proof bookcases if possible. Guard more against physical harm to the book than against its theft, if a choice must be made. Shelving should be particularly smooth surfaced to prevent damage to the binding. Save space in small collections by not using subject classification; a shelf location or simple numbered series will suffice. This allows the books to be shelved in the smallest possible area. For collections too large for a few cases but not large enough for a special room, use iron grilling to set off a section of a stack for such special collections as these.

Nonbook materials

It would be impracticable to attempt a definitive treatment of the proper care of nonbook materials here since the treatments of some of these materials, pamphlets and maps, for example, are complex enough to justify the publication of entire books. A few suggestions regarding the housing and care of the most frequently found nonbook materials are offered.

9

Maps. Cases and files for the storage of maps vary greatly from library to library. Some libraries use several kinds and others use only one type. The TVA Map Division at Knoxville uses a variety of cases, including oversize, legal size, and correspondence size filing cabinets and tracings or blueprint cabinets. Where possible, they have tried to use equipment in which the maps could be kept unfolded. The decision of the Army Map Service to place sets of its map series in libraries designated as depositories has led to a sudden intensification of the problem of adequate map storage. The American Library Association committee on the Army Map Service studied both horizontal and vertical methods of storage and, after pointing out the factors involved, suggested that each library should decide upon the type of unit which best suited the given situation.[7] When maps are frequently consulted, they probably should be laid flat in a blueprint cabinet. Care should be taken that, regardless of the case used, no more maps be put in a single folder or drawer than can be easily located, removed, and refiled.

In instances where the map series is chiefly a problem of storage, as is the case with many of the depository libraries, the legal size filing cabinet may be the most satisfactory solution. This means that many of the maps must be folded, but this need not necessarily damage them. If the maps are printed on good quality paper and are seldom unfolded and refolded, the legal size filing cabinet offers a good and easily accessible place for their preservation. Further, the maps may be folded so that they can be easily opened when they are consulted. When maps are so housed, they should first be put into envelopes or folders in order to make the file contents uniform and easily consulted. The envelope or folder provides a uniform surface for classification numbers or subject headings if the reference-catalog decision is to treat the material in this manner. Geologists often prefer to have specially made, large-drawer, wooden cabinets in which the Geological Survey maps may be conveniently and safely stored. One such smoothly working cabinet has thirty 22-inch by 24-inch drawers for filing maps horizontally and in alphabetical order.

[7]Pierce Butler and Others, "Special Materials: A Symposium," in Herman H. Fussler (ed.), op. cit., p.80.

Map files may be wood or steel, horizontal or vertical, built-in or sectional. The choice of wooden or steel cases will probably be governed by library policy. Horizontal files are more generally used than vertical, although each type has certain advantages. Map cases in the middle of a room should not exceed counter height. Cases over six feet high are somewhat less accessible than those below eye level. Where storage space is at a premium, sectional horizontal files may be stacked to a height of six feet or more. Such map cases accommodate the collections of the U. S. Army Map Service, the National Archives, the Bureau of the Census, and the Library of Congress.[8]

Atlases. Atlases used in reference or reading rooms frequently are housed in cases made of wood finished to blend with the furniture in the room. The shelves may be solid or may be constructed of frames that pull out, drawer-fashion, the full depth of the shelves. In the stack an atlas would be shelved according to its size.

The problem of shelving folio atlases is one to which no perfect solution has yet been found. When large folio atlases are shelved vertically, the weight of their own pages tends to warp the covers and loosen or break the bindings unless they are packed tightly together. Thus tightly confined, there is considerable friction on the bindings whenever they are consulted. There is no agreement about the exact size at which it is no longer safe for a volume to stand vertically on a shelf. Ideally, each folio atlas should lie on a separate roller shelf. If, however, several atlases must occupy the same shelf, the largest should be on the bottom, even though that may place it slightly out of order. When a larger book rests on a smaller one for a time, the former has a tendency to warp, and this should be avoided. Open-bar shelves, such as are found in many libraries for small books should not be used for folio volumes. They cause undue friction on the bindings

---

[8]Clara Egli LeGear, Maps; Their Care, Repair and Preservation in Libraries, U. S. Library of Congress, Reference Department, Division of Maps (Washington: The Library of Congress, 1949), p. 24.

which often frays the covers and breaks corners.[9]

Music. Where use justifies, or preservation demands, scores should be bound and otherwise treated as regular books, if of book size. If thin, commercial pamphlet board bindings are satisfactory. If the score is to be used in a way that requires its having to lie flat, it would be better in many instances to tie it into cardboard folders than to bind as a regular book; however, proper binding of many scores will allow the bound score to lie flat for use. Margins and the thickness of the score are the principal factors here. Thin scores, infrequently used, can be placed in manila folders and filed in vertical filing cabinets. Miniature scores should be bound in cloth or pamphlet bindings. Sheet music is well adapted to satisfactory filing in large vertical files, arranged in the small library simply by title.

Pamphlets. The very small library will find a few pamphlet boxes sufficient to house those items which it wishes to retain and which are not in constant use or are being displayed as timely information on subjects of current interest. The small or medium-sized library will probably need, in addition, vertical file space, in which pamphlets are filed in manila folders arranged alphabetically by subject. This file should be weeded constantly. Most pamphlets which will have very heavy use over a period of years should be bound in cloth or, if of slight proportions, in pamphlet binding and should be cataloged, classified, and otherwise treated as a book. The large library and the special library should make no decisions regarding the complex problem of pamphlets without a study of the subject going vastly beyond the purposes of this chapter. Such libraries are referred to Condit's comprehensive treatment of pamphlets, with which many librarians are already familiar.[10]

Films and microfilm.

...storage...does not require extraordinary precautions. the optimum humidity and temperature for microfilms

[9]Ibid., p. 11.
[10]Lester Condit, A Pamphlet About Pamphlets (Chicago: University of Chicago Press, 1939).

are practically identical with those for books--about 50
per cent relative humidity at 70°F. Freedom from dust
for both projectors and film is important. Microfilm,
all of which is of the safety type, may be kept in specially designed filing cabinets made by several office
equipment companies. It may also be conveniently
stored in shallow trays in metal storage cabinets.
Present types of flat-sheet reproduction may be filed in
vertical files or in file boxes. Since microreproduc-
tions cannot be consulted without optical assistance,
there is no advantage in distributing them by classification with books in a stack; and care of the material
would be difficult under such conditions.[11]...problems
of storing and preserving such materials...have been
greatly exaggerated. In setting up their specifications
for audiovisual aids, the Committee on Planning School
Library Quarters, of the American Association of
School Librarians, has indicated the type of film cabinets, slide cabinets, and record racks it would prefer
to have but has not set up any specific requirements for
the room in which the cabinets and racks are to be
placed. Similarly, the Society of Motion Picture Engi-
neers has experimented to determine the best means of
preserving safety film, which becomes brittle if the
humidity is too low. It has determined the optimum
temperature and humidity and has indicated the various
means by which the best conditions may be assured.
Luckily, the best atmospheric conditions for safety film
are the best conditions also for books.[12]

Recordings. File recordings vertically on racks which
have partitions every four or five inches to prevent too
much lean. In warm and humid climates where heat is
great enough to make warping a possibility, file horizontally.

Architectural potentialities of bookshelves

The architectural potentialities of bookshelves are seldom fully exploited; as a matter of fact, even after all

[11]Butler and Others, op. cit., p.83.
[12]Ibid., p.92.

these centuries of libraries, they can be said to have been little more than explored. To give some indication of the validity of such a generalization, consider a typical reading room in a typical library at almost any time in the modern history of libraries. The reading room is ordinarily planned to hold a certain number of readers and a certain number of books. Crowding (or spreading) chairs, tables, or books is often considered to be the only flexible feature, once the room is an architectural reality. Actually, the range in book and reader capacity is considerable. The arrangement and the amount and type of shelving used in a particular situation can allow for almost unlimited absorption of space which has been provided for growth in the book collection and in reading room use without giving the appearance of housing a scanty collection of books and a few scattered readers. Growth of the collection and growth in the number of readers are often uneven processes; this factor, too, can be made to appear even and normal by judicious use of the proper type of bookshelves. While modular construction may be proving to be the real or fundamental answer to such problems of changing need,[13] to most of us modular construction can serve in the immediate future principally as a source of suggestion along lines of flexibility, or perhaps in connection with renovation and additional construction for an existing structure. Intelligent practice in shelf work can be relied upon to help absorb some of the hazards inherent in the estimates, predictions, guesses, and hopes that go into planning new buildings and additions.

An illustration of the architectural potentialities of bookshelves would be to consider a reading room with a large number of books and readers to accommodate, and the same room with a small number of books and readers. A room 36 feet by 72 feet can house in perfectly comfortable fashion eighty-eight readers and fifteen thousand volumes and still have ample room for the librarian and the furniture and equipment needed for use in a reading room situation. While at first glance this would seem to be a fairly liberal per-reader allowance (29.5 square feet), actually it

---

[13]Donald E. Bean and Ralph E. Ellsworth, Modular Planning for College and Small University Libraries (Iowa City, Ia.: Privately Printed by the Authors, 1948).

is low (21 square feet); for the floor space occupied by the shelving required to house fifteen thousand volumes must be deducted from the total area of the room before the square-feet-per-reader rules of thumb can be applied. The most orderly fashion in which to arrange the shelving in this situation (assuming that the work carried on in the room permitted the arrangement) would be to use one end of the room for a series of double-faced bookcases or ranges, arranged in stack-like order running the long way of the room with one end of each range against the end wall nearest the door (and the librarian). These ranges or bookcases would be only four sections long; there would be six of them on a five-foot-plus center. Together with wall shelving on the other three walls of the room, fifteen thousand volumes and eighty-eight readers could be accommodated without giving a crowded appearance. The stack section would not tend to break up the evenness of the rest of the room, which would have eleven tables, 10 feet by 40 inches, each accommodating eight readers. Oddly enough, if the bookcases were shifted from their stack-like position at one end of the room into an alcove-forming arrangement down one side of the room (with the result that wall shelving on that side would be lost), the room would suddenly look very full of books and bookcases, but would actually accommodate a collection of only approximately two-thirds the size of the first. The alcoves could be equipped with standard tables, have smaller tables, have only chairs, or have no furniture at all, and still be acceptably "furnished" from an aesthetic point of view, thus making the number of readers an extremely flexible item.

Shelf work must not be confused with library building, planning, and architecture, but better planning and better architecture will result when shelving problems and opportunities are recognized, understood, and given full consideration. For example, in the new Massachusetts Institute of Technology Library, the "...main room is divided by shelving and exhibition panels into five bays, in which reading tables and comfortable chairs make an inviting atmosphere."[14] To give illustrations of unfortunate results of ignoring certain shelving problems and opportunities would be merely to echo the general and specific wails of

[14]"M.I.T. Opens New Library," Library Journal, LXXV (1950), 1253.

many librarians in many library buildings.[15] Shelf work can, however, ameliorate or obviate many planning and architectural blunders and, to a reasonable degree, give an "open collection" atmosphere to an ill-conceived modern library structure or to a building which was once a serviceable one, but which now hampers modern forms of service.

Librarians who have done building consultant work have at times found themselves called in to advise on building additions, radical structural changes, or even new buildings, only to discover that some simple device, such as replacing a row of wooden bookcases with a two-tier steel stack unit, thus doubling the library's open shelf book capacity, was all that was needed. Often the librarian on the spot will have thought of such solutions to shelving problems but, as in the case just cited, may have found the ceiling too low, by inches perhaps, to allow the installation to be made. Since librarians are human, it is understandable how a few hundred dollars worth of plaster which could be knocked down in a few hours could have appeared to represent an insurmountable obstacle to solving certain shelving problems. The only solution is often thought to be a new library building or a new wing, with their thousands of dollars worth of foundation, walls, and roof. Frequently, it would be better to strike about more immediately, both figuratively and literally. Nor should the awesome report that the ceiling beams are "structural" or "bearing" or "sustaining" always be allowed to frighten the librarian who is intent upon the business of getting the desired number of books into a particular area. Structural beams can be designed with humps and bends just to suit such situations and can be installed one at a time if, indeed, the whole building is apt to fall down, as the reports would sometimes seem to indicate. The principal idea is to get the shelves where the books ought to be, rather than to be content merely with putting the books where the shelves happen to be. In the process of carrying out this idea, one should not be too readily discouraged by things physical, psychological, or fiscal.

[15]Robert H. Muller, "College Library Buildings Self-Appraised," College and Research Libraries, IX (1948), 221-26.

Chapter 2

PAGING AND SHELVING BOOKS

Paging and circulation

The two most important duties performed by shelf workers are paging and shelving books. Paging takes precedence over all other duties the shelf worker performs, for someone is waiting for the book. Satisfactory paging, however, depends to a large extent upon good shelving, for, if a book has been incorrectly shelved, paging it becomes difficult or impossible.

Although, technically, paging begins when a page is handed a call slip, actually the paging process cannot properly be considered in isolation from circulation procedures. For example, in some libraries a call slip is checked against the general circulation file before it is handed to a page; in others, the page is given the call slip first, and the only call slips that are checked with the general file are those for which books have not been found in their customary places on the shelves. It is necessary, then, to consider paging procedure in the light of circulation procedure. The many circulation systems in operation employ various kinds of equipment and procedures which are now so varied that one can no longer assume, for example, that each book in a library has a book card or, for that matter, that any circulation procedure is common to all libraries.

Search the file or the shelf first? To search the circulation file or the shelf first is a moot question. Most public libraries do not have a file of cards by classification number representing "books not in place on the shelf." For these libraries, then, the only thing to do is to send the page directly to the shelf. In college and university libraries practice as to which is done first varies considerably. Often within a single library one procedure is used for a few years and then the other. When one reader presents several call slips, the problem becomes more complex. Which is better (or worse) for the reader: (1) to waste his time while all his call slips are being checked with the file, even though many of the books requested are on the shelf, or (2) to waste his time while a page checks the shelves for a book which is out or is located temporarily in some other place when he might have had his report immediately from circulation's check of the general file?

To determine which procedure it should use a library can run tests. If most of the books requested by the average reader are usually found on the shelf, the file should not be checked first. If most of the books wanted by the average reader are not usually found on the shelf, but their location is indicated by the general circulation file, the file should be checked first. The time factor, however, must also be considered. It may take several minutes to check the shelves in some large libraries, but only a fraction of that time to check the circulation file, while the reverse may be true in another library. The physical aspects of the building, the type and treatment of the collection, and other local conditions will also affect the decision.

Notice author and title when paging. If the call slip gives the author and title as well as the call number, and many of them do, it is highly desirable to train pages to think of the book being paged in terms of what book and by whom, especially if the book bearing the call number requested is not to be found in its regular place on the shelf. The book might be shelved only slightly out of place but be noticed if the page is also thinking of author and title. Too strict an adherence to the idea of bringing only the book bearing the precise call number designated may lead to such absurdities as reporting a book "not on shelf" when actually there is another copy there. The page should disregard the copy number when the reader has written it on the call slip. Most pages readily learn to notice author and title.

A different book on the same subject? Another step that a page can sometimes take is to bring the reader a different book on the same subject if the one requested is out. Pages should never be told to do this unless the book selected is to be turned over to a professional worker at circulation, who may or may not wish to recommend it to the reader. However, it is surprising and very satisfying to see what an excellent job some of the better pages can do. Experienced, intelligent, and interested pages, properly taught, can be of real help to the reader and to circulation in this respect. The safeguard here, of course, is the fact that a professional assistant at the circulation desk will often know from previous experience, first, whether to encourage this practice and, second, how to make the specific decision as to whether a particular substitute will be offered a particular reader.

Whether or not pages are to be encouraged to bring "some other good book on the subject" is a decision which hinges to some extent upon the type of library concerned and reader served. While many public and college libraries might find this practice readily acceptable, it should be employed with discretion in the research library, although even in the research library not every title requested is for a specific research use. It is revealing to notice how often even the best of scholars merely want a good book on a particular subject, presumably, of course, when they are not working in their restricted subject fields.

Stationing pages. If the stacks are equipped with mechanical devices, such as automatic book carriers, pneumatic tubes, telautograph, telephones, etc., it may be best to station the pages on particular floor levels and have them do both paging and shelving. If the stacks are not so equipped, but have an elevator, the pages may be best stationed at or near the circulation desk. Brown and Bousfield offer the following suggestion:

> If there are not over seven tiers of stacks, and if the loan desk is located on the same level as the fourth tier, it will probably be found more desirable to station the attendants at the loan desk.[1]

If pages are assigned to certain floors and are to shelve on those floors when not paging, the stacks should be equipped with colored signal lights so that the page will know a call slip has arrived at his stack level station and that he should

[1]Charles H. Brown and H. G. Bousfield, Circulation Work in College and University Libraries. Chicago: American Library Association, 1933, p.66.

stop shelving and page the book at once. Bells, buzzers, and other stack installations which would disturb the carrel user or any reader in the stacks should seldom, if ever, be installed.

Time required to page a book. Many studies have been made attempting to establish the length of time that should be required to deliver a book from the stacks to the loan desk. Such studies have done little to establish a standard, because proper distinctions were not drawn between requests for one title or several titles, which might or might not be scattered over the several stack levels. Obviously, if a reader wants seven books all of which will be found on one range of a particular stack level, the time required by a single page will be much less than that required to secure seven titles in various classifications scattered over a seven-tier stack, particularly if the pages are stationed at the circulation desk rather than on the various stack levels. Because of the lack of these refinements in the investigations which have been made, no attempt is made here to set up any particular standard. Brown and Bousfield feel that any library system requiring over three minutes to deliver the average book might investigate its procedure to advantage.[2]

A time clock may be used to keep a check on the time taken to page a book. Some libraries clock every call slip. Other libraries keep paging-time records only for short periods at regular or varying intervals. Those which clock all slips usually do so because it is felt that this serves as a constant impetus to greater speed in paging.

Assigning call slips to pages. In systems where the pages are stationed at the circulation desk (and this probably includes most libraries) it is a more efficient procedure to give the call slips for particular stack levels to certain pages and those for other stack levels to certain other pages, rather than to give to a single page all the call slips presented by a single reader. This would not be true, however, if it results in having several pages going to the stacks for a single reader. The procedure recommended should be used only when the traffic is very heavy and only a few minutes elapse between readers submitting call slips. It is much more economical in time and energy to have one

[2]Ibid., p.72.

page go to upper level stacks to get the books from that area for several readers and another page go to the lower stack levels than it is to have each page go both up and down. This would appear to be so obvious that it need not be mentioned, but there are many libraries in which the practice is, and has been for years, to hand all the call slips for one reader to one page, even though it takes the page to many different levels and slows down services considerably.

Use of elevators in paging. Because traffic is often so heavy that much time is wasted waiting for elevators, pages, staff, and readers should usually be requested not to use elevators for floors adjacent to the delivery area unless they have a very heavy load of books to carry or have a book truck to move. This practice not only lightens the elevator load, but it speeds service a great deal. Climbing the eight feet of stairway from one stack level to another does not work a hardship upon the pages.

Missing books

Searching for missing books. The most frequent and perplexing problem in paging is that of missing books. Most libraries have had to develop searching routines to be followed in case a book is not in its place on the shelf and there is no record of it to be found in the general circulation file. A printed or typed copy of the searching routine for the library should be given to each page, and each step, together with the reason for it, explained to him.

Kellam's article on tracing misplaced books is one of the most detailed studies published on this subject.[3] As he points out, the search always begins with checking the shelf list. This is done to verify the call number and to obtain information concerning the correctness of author and title, number of copies, accession numbers, and, in case the shelf list is used for inventory record, to see if copies have been marked "discarded" or "missing." The search than continues through the shelves in the stack, the temporary shelves on the stack levels, the sorting shelves, mending shelves, new book shelves, and snag shelves. Of course

[3]W. P. Kellam, "Tracing Misplaced Books in a University Library," Library Journal, LVIII (1933), 155-56.

the general circulation file and temporary files are rechecked. Missing books are often located in departmental
libraries, departmental offices, or private offices of pro-
fessors. Frequently they are "missing" through failure to
charge them or to record the permanent location in the
catalog or shelf list. This enumeration by no means ex-
hausts the potential list of possible places a missing book
(or record of its location) might be found. A report covering a period of eighty-four days and showing where the
missing books were finally located is included in Mr.
Kellam's study. It gives a very good picture of where
missing books are likely to be found. In addition to indicating places to look for missing books, the study also shows
the relative importance of each of these places. From such
a study made locally any library could make up an excellent routine for tracing its missing books. The results of
Kellam's study are shown in the table[4] below.

$$\text{Located} \ldots \ldots 651$$
$$\text{Not located} \ldots \ldots 168$$

$$\text{Total traced} \ldots 819$$
$$\text{Per cent located} \ldots 80-$$

These were located in the following places:

On shelf in stacks	.90
In circulation files	.66
Unfiled circulation	111
On sorting shelf	.56
Wrong call number	.67
Misplaced	.55
On shelf in stack	47
Circulation file	8
Cataloging errors	4
From shelf list	.39
Lost	11
Missing at inventory	24
Discarded	4
Mending	.10
Miscarded	4

[4]Ibid., p.156.

On reserve without dummy in circulation file 5
Reserve dummy incorrect 1
In departmental libraries and not noted in catalog 4
Hold shelf. 4
New shelf 1
Relabeling. 4
Process of cataloging and marking incomplete. 2
Labeled incorrectly 3
Other reasons included 15
Found later (after first searches) 110
   On shelf. 37
   In circulation 57
   On sorting shelf 1
   On snag shelf 5
   Returned later 10

Missing books record. The record of missing books
kept by a library is derived principally from two sources:
(1) books which are found missing in inventory and (2)
books currently in demand which cannot be located when
requested. Both types of missing books should be searched
periodically, but a file of the missing books currently in
demand should be kept by the shelf department. This can
be done conveniently by filing the original call slips in
class or stack order. Such a file is not one to be built up
and retained solely for aimless further search by the shelf
worker. It can become one of the most important records
of the shelf department, for it is a selective, continuous inventory of missing books currently in demand. It contains
information of value for the stack supervisor, the circulation chief, the order department, and the library administrator. It should be checked periodically, and decisions
made regarding replacement, withdrawal, etc., of the
missing items.

Shelving and circulation

Comparing discharged slips and books. Just as paging
begins, theoretically, when the page is handed a call slip,
so shelving begins, theoretically, when a book has been discharged by circulation or is received from the catalog department. Again, however, we find that the two processes
cannot be so arbitrarily segregated. For example, the

first step in shelving a discharged book is to check it against the card which has been withdrawn from the circulation charge file. This card may be a book card or a call slip depending upon the circulation system used in a given library. This comparison of discharged books and their book cards or call slips may be done either by circulation assistants or by the shelf workers. In some systems the practice is to have either do it, depending upon which has the most time. As a matter of fact, this comparison of books and cards (or slips) is a very good common-ground activity because it gives both pages and circulation assistants something worthwhile to do when they are not occupied with more important duties. (If the percentage of error in discharging is very low, slipping would not normally be checked.) The discharged books are next placed on return shelves, sorting tables, or book trucks.

Return shelves, sorting shelves, and book trucks. If return shelves or tables are used, they should be near the circulation desk and must be ample enough to allow for rough classification (100's, 200's, etc.) and to hold any maximum accumulation of books which is likely to occur. Some shelf supervisors object to "return shelves" or "retention shelves" and even to "sorting shelves" because books seem to stay there and cause many missing-book reports. In some public libraries, however, the return shelf is very popular with readers. Again this is a question which should be decided on its own merits locally. Some stack supervisors object to sorting tables, while others do not see how sorting could be done without them. Using window ledges, carrels, etc. for holding the books on their various routes back to the shelf can be prevented by strict adherence to regulations which prohibit placing books anywhere except on the specified return shelves and book trucks. Modernly equipped stacks have station desks or shelves where books returned on the book conveyor are sorted and kept until they are to be shelved.

If book trucks are used instead of return shelves, circulation assistants should arrange the books on them in approximate stack order to avoid the necessity of having to empty, sort, and re-load each truck. A general policy to have the book always on a truck during the entire process of shelving, from the time it is discharged until the shelver is ready to place it on the shelf will result usually in better

service with a great deal less confusion, less misunder-
standing, and less irritation on the part of those who have
to page the books.

Assignment of shelving areas. Shelving should be a
continuous process, but not all pages should be assigned to
shelving, for it is a much more difficult process than paging. A good practice is to assign the shelving for a certain
area to a particular individual, adjusting the size of the
area to the work load. Where temporary fluctuations may
require it, a shelver with a light work load may be asked to
assist in an area where shelving is heavy. Such a worker
should be temporarily under the supervision of the shelver
ordinarily assigned to that area. Nonobservance of this
policy will lead to a sense of indifference on the part of
shelvers, for no one can maintain a high sense of responsibility for work over which he has no control. Too frequent
reassignment of areas of responsibility will destroy a
"pride in ownership" attitude to which the shelver is not
only entitled, but which he should by all means be encouraged to cultivate. This idea can hardly be carried too far,
and should the supervisor himself shelve books in an assigned area, he might seriously consider placing the books
on the shelves on their fore edges subject to revision by
the person responsible for that area.

Shelving and binding

Shelf workers should be trained to call to the attention
of the supervisor books which they consider to be in need
of binding or repair. The supervisor will work in close
cooperation with the reference department and the circulation department (of which he is probably a staff member)
regarding the timeliness of withdrawing particular books
or sets from active use. He will then see that the books
are properly charged and sent on to the department or the
person responsible for binding or binding preparations,
according to the particular library's practice. Actually,
there is no real reason why the books themselves need to
be handled at the circulation desk to be charged to the
bindery as long as the charges are forwarded for all books
taken from the shelves. It is necessary, however, that
books returned from the bindery be routed through circulation to be discharged. Another procedure is to make a

duplicate charge card for each title sent to the bindery, placing the original charge card in the general circulation file and the duplicate in a separate file representing all the books currently charged to "bindery." The latter file is usually kept by the staff responsible for binding. As books are returned from the bindery, they are first discharged from this file, permitting discharge from the general circulation file by means of the duplicate card rather than from the books. However, the safer and simpler process is to discharge bindery returns at circulation directly from the books. There should always be a record in the general circulation file of the cataloged books which are at the bindery. Merely keeping a separate file for books at the bindery is seldom satisfactory.

The shelf work supervisor should work in close collaboration with the person in charge of binding and repair, because books can and should be fed from the shelves into the bindery under controls regarding time, amount of material, budgetary allowance, and nature of the work at a given time. If there is no binding or repair specialist on the staff, a situation which will exist in many libraries, the shelf-work supervisor is a logical person to make some study of the care and repair of books. If there is a bindery, the supervisor should still possess considerable knowledge concerning the care, repair, and binding of books, and he should attempt to teach as much of this knowledge as he can to his shelf workers.

Shelving techniques

As the shelver goes about his work, he should straighten shelves constantly, pulling the books forward on the shelf and then pushing the protruding ones back even with the others until they all stand in a straight row, their spines even with the front of the shelf. At the same time, he should shift them to the left side of the shelf to eliminate "lean," and use the book support which should be at the right of each partly filled shelf of books to draw the books snugly together. Despite all that can be said for always keeping every shelf just like this, experience will show that it is unnecessary and undesirable to push all the books to the left side when a shelf is practically full and the only gaps are those representing the place where a book cur-

26 Paging and shelving

rently in circulation belongs. Such a situation does not make for continued lean, and the books are not therefore damaged. Shelves too tightly packed should be relieved by shifting a volume or two to the next shelf.

Shelvers must be taught that books must not be left loose, uneven, or leaning on a shelf, or damage will result, and yet that they should not be handled unnecessarily. The veteran shelver knows at a glance where to draw the line, and others should be taught, for the line does need to be drawn. As far as possible, specific instructions should be placed in the hands of shelf workers, especially where old or fragile books and bindings are involved.

Chapter 3

SHIFTING AND MOVING BOOKS

Where space is available and a collection is merely expanding onto additional shelves, shifting books is a fairly simple process. Where a library is being moved into a new building or where a collection is being shifted into open shelves or divisional arrangements or being combined with collections previously housed in separate rooms or other buildings, moving and shifting books becomes a major problem. It is possible to move a very large collection without having any book unavailable to the public for more than a few hours. The move into the new Princeton Library, for example, was planned so that there would be a minimum of interruption to library use.[1]

Planning

The earlier planning is under way, the more effective any eventual move will be, for definite, detailed plans must be prepared before a move takes place. In small libraries the librarian himself may be chiefly responsible for planning and supervising the moving. In larger libraries where direct supervision by the head librarian is not so essential, the authority is sometimes delegated to another individual or to a committee. When the Enoch Pratt Free Library was moved from its temporary quarters into its new building, a director was secured for the project. He and the various department heads prepared the general specifications for the move, on the basis of which bids were received and the contract was awarded. The same group, in a series of conferences, prepared a moving schedule which

[1]Frederick S. Osborne, "New Library 'Humanistic Laboratory'," Library Journal, LXXIII (1948), 1763-71; Lionel James Lee, "Always So Much to Move!" Library Journal, LXXV (1950), 534-537.

was finally adopted as the working plan.[2] At Pennsylvania State College and at Princeton, committees were appointed to plan the transfer of books and equipment. The committees were composed of representatives from the departments of administration, circulation, reference, and (at Penn State) from the catalog department.

The basic information needed for planning to shift a collection should include: (1) the number of sections or shelves of books in each subject classification; (2) the number of sections or shelves available on each tier; (3) decisions regarding the new locations of the several classes of books; and (4) decisions regarding distribution of free space among the various classes.

By establishing a simple relation between the number of books to be shelved on each tier and the amount of space available, the amount of free space to be allotted can be determined. Free space may be utilized either by leaving top or bottom shelves empty or by leaving a certain amount of space unoccupied on each shelf. (The continuity of closed sets or consecutively numbered volumes of any set or run should not be broken in order to leave space on a particular shelf.) Free space should be left at the end of each major break in the classification. Attention should also be given to the fact that some classes of books grow more rapidly than others. Since oversize books are usually filed in a separate sequence, special provision must be made for them. Periodicals require special attention, and space should be provided for a minimum of five years' growth wherever possible.

One plan[3] for a major shift began with duplicate drawings of floor plans for each stack level. A large scale was used (1/4 inch to the foot) so there would be ample space for indicating the inclusive classification numbers for each section. A general plan for dividing the book collection among the several floors was then made, based on a count of the number of sections occupied by each classification. It was found desirable to put these figures, as well as the capacities of each stack level, on a separate sheet since

[2]Lloyd W. Josselyn, "Moving the Enoch Pratt Library," Library Journal, LVIII (1933), 480-82.
[3]William E. Jorgensen, "Rearranging Book Collection," Library Journal, LXVI (1941), 570-71.

this helped in explaining the shifting. Finally, using the duplicate plans, the new location for each class of books was written in the spaces representing each section. It was decided to leave some space vacant on each shelf in order to prolong the time before another shift would be necessary. The amount of space left on each shelf was determined by dividing the amount of free space by the total space available. Assuming that a particular stack level contains 150 sections and that 120 sections of books are to be shelved on this level, there would be 30 sections of free shelf space. These 30 sections, divided by the total space, 150 sections, allows for 20 per cent free space, which may be distributed as desired.

The procedure followed at the Toledo Public Library provides an example of what is involved in preparing for a move.[4] This move was complicated by the need for increasing the number of subject service areas from four to eleven and intershelving a number of branch library collections. Horizontally perforated, colored, gummed labels were made to use in identifying related subject areas: yellow signified art, music, and the humanities; green, history, travel, and biography, etc. Each service head was made responsible for measuring his collections in the old building. In addition, estimates of the amount of space required for expansion of each collection were made and added to the measurements of the collections. This total was then measured on the shelves in the new building and, since the shelves were numbered with chalk, a notation was made of the inclusive numbers of shelves to be occupied.

The day before the actual moving started, the proper colored labels were affixed by the narrow portion above the perforation to the individual wooden shelves beneath the volumes in the old building. Each of these labels bore in pencil the number of the shelf in the new building. Thus when the movers packed a shelf of books in the container, retaining the proper sequence of books on the shelf, they had only to tear the label off, moisten the back of it, and affix it to the end of the box. By its color it showed to which service area the con-

[4]Russell J. Schunk, "Librarian's Nightmare," Library Journal, LXVI (1941), 817-21.

tainer should be sent, and upon which shelf the books should be placed when unpacked.[5]

Equipment and methods

As soon as the new locations have been agreed upon, the equipment and methods to be used in moving the books must be determined. In the main stack book trucks may constitute the only necessary equipment, but if the shifting must cover any considerable distance, using boxes should be considered. They may increase the rate of speed with which the reshelving can be done and will reduce the hazard to which the books are exposed if moved by hand. Equipment used in moving books has varied from miscellaneous assortments of cardboard boxes to specially made felt-lined wooden boxes and steel roller conveyors. In the Toledo Public Library, where a shelf of books was considered as the unit in moving, special containers of corrugated cardboard were used because of possible danger to books and to the floors of the new building. These boxes were made in two sizes, the one for standard-size books being 36 inches long, 10-1/2 inches wide, and 9 inches deep, and the one for large books, 36 inches long, 15 inches wide, and 12 inches deep. All had regular flap covers so that the books could be protected from the weather.[6] At Pennsylvania State College wooden boxes measuring 38 inches by 14 inches by 12 inches were used, since that size, because of the many oversize volumes, seemed most efficient.[7] During the general shifting and moving at Brown University in 1938-40, boxes 3 feet in length requiring two men for handling were discarded and replaced by boxes made of half-inch pine with inside measurements of 1 foot by 1 foot by 8 inches. Since one worker could carry two of these, the new boxes increased by one-half foot the number of books each person was able to carry. When filled, a box of this size balanced itself so that it could be carried by its edge without spilling the books. A human chain was used to forward the boxes of books from

[5]Ibid., p.818.
[6]Ibid., p.818.
[7]Katharine M. Stokes and Margaret F. Knoll, "Moving the Pennsylvania State College Library," Wilson Library Bulletin, XVI (1941), 230-38.

packer to shelver.[8] Once the books actually begin to move, additional problems present themselves. Since the speed of the individual shelver is necessarily that of an entire crew, any element which decreases his speed lessens the efficiency of the process. The one foot of books each of these boxes contained constitutes the maximum a shelver can handle in one movement with reasonable speed and accuracy.

Methods employed in moving books frequently differ since the moving procedure is often based on the service areas which are to be included in the new locations. The move at Denison University, complicated by the problem of having to bring books in from almost every building on the campus, was carefully planned a year in advance. Since the new building was quite near the old, it was possible to build a chute from both the second and first floors of the old building to the stone terrace of the new. Twenty boxes were built, measuring 39-1/2 inches by 11-1/2 inches by 9-1/2 inches. This size box was chosen because each could accommodate the books on a single shelf of the old library. The boxes had reinforced handles and were numbered consecutively. When loaded with books they were too heavy and cumbersome for one person to carry, so the students worked in teams, each team being assigned to certain boxes so that the numerical order could be maintained. There was no confusion at either end of the move. Fourteen boys were employed, four being assigned to packing and getting the boxes down the chutes and ten being used to carry the boxes to their locations in the new building. In addition, two staff members were posted at each end of the move to supervise and to keep figures on the rate of the moving. The books were moved from one location at a time because the librarian felt that several teams working from a number of places would cause confusion. Those volumes which had been stored in other buildings were boxed and brought to the library in a truck. All of the books were dusted before they were moved, and the shelves in the new building were washed and dried before the books were placed on them.[9]

Some libraries, especially those in metropolitan areas,

[8]William H. Jesse, "Moving Books," Library Quarterly, XI (1941), 328-33.
[9]Annie L. Craigie, "Moving Day," Library Journal, LXIII (1938), 388-89.

engage professional moving organizations to move their equipment and collections. When a rapid move is necessary, as may be the case in libraries where use is continuous, the employment of professional movers may be more satisfactory than attempting to move with library personnel alone.

Chapter 4

STACK MANAGEMENT
AND SHELVING EQUIPMENT

The bookstack

Only in the small library can the entire book collection be effectively serviced in a single central reading area fully open to all patrons. Wider use of the library and increased book resources introduce problems of adequate storage for those volumes which are less in demand. Volumes most frequently used must be selected from the total collection and made readily available. Some public libraries attempt to meet the urgency of the problem by discarding outdated and unused materials. Until recently, however, the bookstack has provided almost the only satisfactory solution to the problem of additional space for the growing collections. The bookstack and most of the work done in it are responsibilities of the shelf-work supervisor.

Definition of terms. Before describing the physical organization of the typical bookstack, a few technical terms should be defined: A section is a vertical series of shelves, usually seven, between two supporting columns. A range is a series of sections, either double or single-faced, placed end to end. A tier, also called floor or stack level, consists of all the ranges, both double and single-faced, placed in a parallel manner on a single level of the stack. Deck refers to the stack tier and includes its service equipment. The book stacks or stack (the library storage space) is usually a distinct building unit structurally, and is here considered as a series of superimposed tiers, though the term "stack" may be used for a single tier.

Construction of stack. The stack is generally self-supporting with the floor loads being carried by a specially constructed metal framework which extends from the basement to the roof with stack floors arranged at intervals of 7 or 7-1/2 feet. Frequently these stack levels are so designed that two decks may be provided for each regular floor. In a few libraries, vertical expansion, planned in advance by the installation of strong foundations and stack columns, has resulted in actual stack towers.

Bookstack not merely storage space. Today in many public libraries, college libraries, and university or research libraries, the bookstack is an essential unit of the complex structure into which the modern library building has evolved. Justification of its existence cannot ordinarily be made simply from the fact that it is a central storehouse for the care and preservation of printed materials; it must also be administered in such a manner as to make its contents promptly and easily available.

Location of the stack is of primary importance from the standpoint of both convenience and future expansion. Current library planning, in line with present educational stress, is increasingly emphasizing convenience for readers. The general trend is to seek some method for a more satisfactory and spontaneous relationship than now exists between readers and books with reading and storage areas completely separate. The location of the stack in existing and proposed buildings has been broken down roughly into six classifications--rear of buildings, center of buildings, beneath reading rooms, around reading rooms, in the reading rooms, and among the reading rooms.[1] The first is recognized as the most common and is the type most easily expanded when additional storage space becomes necessary. Since the need for natural light in the stack has been successfully challenged, the stack area has moved from periphery to the center of the building, permitting a more compact arrangement. Unfortunately, the central core stack, though it may be satisfactory for years, eventually becomes full. The inflexibility of central stacks often makes a new building necessary long before this should be the case. The libraries of the Universities of Colorado and Nebraska are housed in buildings which combine the characteristics of a permanent stack area at the rear of the building with large, free access, storage areas closely related to the reading rooms.

[1]Leroy Charles Merritt, "The Book Stock," in Herman H. Fussler (ed.), Library Buildings for Library Service. Chicago: American Library Association, 1947, p.62-66.

Flexibility. The stack installation that seems to satisfy the requirements of both flexibllity and expansibility is the "among the reading rooms" type. The new libraries at Princeton, Washington State, Bradley University, and Hardin-Simmons University, and the plans for the State University of Iowa and North Dakota Agricultural College follow this pattern, using modular construction.[2] These libraries have almost completely flexible interiors which can be arranged to accommodate any library function-- processing, readers' services, or book storage.

Stack capacity

Formulas for size of stack. In addition to location, the stack dimensions and the number of volumes which such areas hold are items which are vital to the stack supervisor. He will need to be almost as well versed in matters pertaining to them as is a library architect or building consultant. Gerould suggested that the stack area of a new library be equal to twice the number of books which will be in the library when it is opened and, if the collection is crowded in its old quarters, from a quarter to a third more space be added to the size of the collection and that the total be doubled in order to provide for the future.[3] Some have used the formula of fifteen volumes per square foot of floor space, a figure which includes space occupied by aisles, elevators, and stairways, but it is considered inadequate for a working collection. Ten volumes per square foot of floor space, including space for aisles, elevators, and stairways, has been found more satisfactory.[4] Henderson discards the formula of fifteen volumes per square foot[5] in favor of his own "cubook," a term which he defines as "...the volume of space required to shelve the

[2]Robert H. Muller, "Library Building Construction Among Colleges and Universities, 1950," College and Research Libraries, XI (1950), 259-261.

[3]James Thayer Gerould, The College Library Building, Its Planning and Equipment. Chicago: American Library Association, 1932, p.33.

[4]Edna Ruth Hanley, College and University Library Buildings. Chicago: American Library Association, 1939, p.17.

[5]Robert W. Henderson, "The Cubook," American Library Association Bulletin, XXXIV (1940), 730-31.

average size book in a typical library."[6] By allowing
eleven cubooks per square foot or 1.5 cubooks per cubic
foot, a rough estimate of stack area may be made. These
figures include space occupied by ranges, all aisles,
stairs, and elevators. Other formulas, based on the shelf-
content or sections, have been devised to estimate the
amount of necessary stack space. Wheeler and Githens
suggest six volumes per linear foot of shelf as being fairly
safe in computing practical working capacity.[7] Randall
recommends seven books to the linear foot as the maximum
safe estimate in a college or university library.[8] Randall
and Gerould agree in stating that the formula of fifty volumes per running foot of single-faced shelving is frequently
used. Both of them point out, however, that close adherence to the formula probably will result in overcrowding.

The "cubook." Henderson's cubook may also be used
for calculating space in terms of book capacity. Allowing
10 per cent for end space, his study[9] showed that one
hundred "average" books almost exactly filled one standard
section, 3 feet long by 7-1/2 feet high. The cubook is based
on estimates by Gerould, modified by counts in the New
York Public Library and the Library of Yale University,
which showed the ratio of the number of books in size
groups to be as follows: octavos 85 per cent, quartos 13
per cent, and folios 2 per cent.[10] The cubook, then, can
express the exact amount of shelf space but indicates only
approximate volumes.

When is a shelf full? A shelf may be considered full
when only three fourths of its ultimate capacity is utilized.
When a shelf is literally filled there is a strain not only on
the books themselves, but on the quality of shelving which
is done. It is maddening to have to try to fit a new acqui-
sition into the remaining one-half inch of shelf space in an

[6]Robert W. Henderson, "Bookstack Planning with the Cubook," Library
Journal, LXI (1936), 52.

[7]Joseph L. Wheeler and Alfred M. Githens, The American Public Library
Building. Chicago: American Library Association, 1941, p.414-15.

[8]William M. Randall, "The Physical Administration of the Book Collection,"
in The American School and University. 8th ed.; New York: American School
Publishing Corp., 1936, p.263.

[9]Henderson, "Bookstack Planning with the Cubook," op. cit., p.52-54.

[10]Henderson, "The Cubook: a Suggested Unit for Bookstack Measure-
ment," Library Journal, LIX (1934), 866-67.

already overcrowded section and to realize that the nearest available space is at least a section away. To place a new series of volumes in an out-of-the-way place decreases the efficiency of the staff members who are responsible for knowing its location, even though a charge card be placed in the circulation file.

Bookshelving

Steel shelving vs. wooden shelving. The structural use of steel in the multi-tier stack practically eliminates the use of wooden shelving in such areas (although makeshift arrangements with wooden shelves and plain boards have met many an emergency). When a steel shelf must be moved, it may be done by simply removing it from its slot or notch and raising or lowering it as the case may be. In (standard) wooden shelving, four shelf pins or supports must be changed after the shelf has been removed and before it can be replaced. Wooden ranges offer a possible fire hazard while the metal equipment does not. Furthermore steel shelving lasts longer. Wooden shelving is suitable for reference and reading rooms because of its ornamental qualities. The advantages of wooden shelving over steel shelving for school libraries seem to have been well established.[11]

Bracket type shelving. Most shelving in the stack areas is designed to provide for the care and preservation of as many volumes as possible. This approach has led to the development of several steel stack types, the two in most common use being the bracket and the standard. The bracket type is characterized by rectangular stack columns in which slots are punched at regular intervals to permit the insertion of key extrusions on the ends of the shelves. This provides a shelf space that, because of vertical shelf-ends and the close interlocking of the shelf to its supporting column, has smooth surfaces that prevent damage to books. It is flexible, too, in that any section can accommodate shelves of varying depth (fore edge to rear edge). A variant of the bracket type is so constructed that the vertical

[11]Charles Daniel, "Bookshelving in the High School Library," University of Illinois Library School Occasional Papers, No. IV [Urbana]: 1949, p. 2 (Mimeographed.)

supporting column is completely sealed and prevents the accumulation of dust. The shelf itself may be of a single sheet or of open bars.

Standard type shelving. The standard stack, sometimes described as the wide-upright type, has structural columns to which are bolted wide sheet metal uprights. These have horizontal slots to take shelves of a certain depth. The horizontal slots make adjustment of the shelves a simpler matter than that provided by the bracket type. The shelf itself, of solid metal, has no projections upon which a book may be damaged. Standard shelving also has another meaning, regardless of the stack type, and often refers to shelf and section dimensions, measurements that have become "standardized."

Shelf dimensions. Bookshelves in most stacks are usually 3 feet long, measured from center to center of shelf supports, and are 8 inches, 10 inches, and 12 inches in depth, depending upon the size of the books to be housed. Sections are made 7 feet or 7-1/2 feet high from floor to floor, usually the latter in order to allow space for seven shelves of books.

Height of shelving and width of aisles. Equipment companies can supply stack sections of special heights. The new Princeton Library, as an example, adopted ceiling heights of 8 feet, 4 inches, for its below-ground-level stack areas. With the growing trend to combine reader and stack areas there has been an increase in the popularity of an 8-foot height. The flexibility and accessibility of the shelves is closely related to the width of the range aisles. If the books in a collection are small, a narrow aisle may be satisfactory; for a general collection a wider aisle is better, since this allows for deeper shelves where necessary. Ranges may be placed as closely as 48 inches apart on range centers when they are to be equipped with 8-inch shelves, but for the general collection a 52-inch or 54-inch center-to-center aisle with 8-inch or 10-inch shelves is preferable. If full advantage is to be taken of the flexibility of an installation, such as the bracket type stack, even wider aisles would be better, especially if the public is to have access to the stack.

Shelving for oversize books. Books may be considered as being in two main groups as far as shelving is concerned, those which can be shelved vertically and those which should be laid on their sides. The smaller, if shelf space is to be used economically, must be divided into two groups, octavos and quartos. The octavos fit easily into a standard 7-1/2-foot section with seven, and frequently eight, shelves. The quartos usually have to be placed on larger shelves. Some libraries which have notched vertical stack columns have additional strips at the bottom of each section so that two shelves of quarto materials can be shelved near the classes to which they belong. Oversize shelving is frequantly provided in connection with carrels. Deep counter-height shelves, such as the atlas cases at the University of Illinois, give privacy to the carrel occupant and provide adequate storage for the larger volumes requiring special care.

Van Hoesen and Kilpatrick measured the heights of 350,000 volumes in the library at Brown in an effort to determine how stack space might be used more economically.[12] Though heights varied within each subject field, they set up three oversize groups: from 26 to 33 centimeters, from 33 to 45 centimeters, and over 45 centimeters. The first two groups were shelved vertically in a separate sequence at the rear of the stack. The third group, the folios, were placed on roller shelves. This system of shelving increased shelf capacity 10 per cent. Van Hoesen and Kilpatrick concluded that:

> Neither the 7-1/2- nor the 8-foot stack is the correct height for shelving 26 cm. books with the best economy of space. A stack tier of seven shelves should be between 86 and 88 inches high (books, clearance, shelves, 80-1/2 inches; floor and base, 5-1/2 - 7-1/2 inches), while one of eight shelves should be between 97 and 100 inches (books, clearance, shelves, 92 inches; floor and base 5 - 8 inches).[13]

Tilting and lighting lower shelves. Some libraries have made use of tilted shelves in order to make it easier to find particular titles shelved on the two lower shelves and in order to increase the circulation of books on the

[12]Norman L. Kilpatrick and Henry B. Van Hoesen, ''The Heights of Three Hundred and Fifty Thousand Volumes,'' Library Quarterly, V(1935), 341-47.
[13]Ibid., p.347.

bottom shelves of open access collections. A study made
at the Gary Public Library showed a correlation between
tilting the lower shelves and the distribution of books circulated from the test sections. All of the sections were
located in the central fiction room and were open to the
public. The books in those sections which were most accessible had a high circulation. When the lower shelves of
those same sections were tilted, a slightly higher usage
was observed. Another factor was that of lighting. Tilting
the lower shelves doubled the amount of light reflected
from them, and circulation increased. Bad lighting had a
reverse effect. Tilted shelves with adequate lighting are
helpful in making book titles more visible and in allowing
for distributing selections over all the shelves in a section
without discriminating against certain titles.[14]

Methods of tilting shelves. Tilted shelves, rubber
stripped to prevent books from slipping backward, are used
with success in a number of libraries. Currently used
shelf types can be adapted to make tilted shelves. With
some wooden shelving it is necessary only to lower the
rear shelf pins. The standard (wide-upright) shelf seems
to present a problem, but by putting the shelf in upside
down one achieves a kind of solution. The book rests on
the front flange and the insertion of a wooden strip against
the back flange prevents its slipping backward. This particular device has been used at the New Haven Public
Library. A tilted shelf is easily obtained with the bracket
type. The shelf is pulled forward at the bottom and a strip
of wood is inserted to hold the shelf and the books on it in
this forward position. Nails are driven into the ends of the
strip of wood to prevent slipping. Since the protruding
portion of the nail is slipped into the bracket slots, damage
to books and equipment is prevented. For the bottom shelf,
a thicker strip is needed in order to give a steeper slope.
Cast iron shelving presents no difficulty; the back of the
shelf can be lowered to another row of rear perforations
to give it the right slope.[15]

[14]Ralph R. Shaw, "The Influence of Sloping Shelves on Book Circulation,"
Library Quarterly, VIII (1938), 480-90.
[15]Willis K. Stetson, "How to Tilt Shelves," Wilson Library Bulletin, XIV
(1940), 402.

Stack control

Elevator and booklift. The physical aspects of the stack have a direct bearing upon the degree of efficiency with which it can be administered. In any multitier stack an elevator or an electric booklift is essential, the elevator being much more desirable than the booklift, if a choice must be made. Both are essential if the library is very large and there are more than seven stack levels. They provide rapid service links between the book-storage and book-use areas. They must be large and sturdy enough to care for big and heavy loads. Without them adequate service could not be achieved in a large library, though a small and compact library can render good service without such mechanical devices.

Use of elevator. In libraries where at least a semiclosed stack was envisioned at the time of construction, the trend toward the open stack has often resulted in complications in the use of the elevator. The elevator is frequently used by students, and this use tends to disrupt service routines. In order to insure an even flow of books coming from and returning to the stack, elevator use must often be regulated. At the University of Illinois, pages are asked not to use the elevators unless they are to go more than three stack levels from their stations. As was pointed out in Chapter 2, in many libraries it is understood that pages will not use the elevator when going to floors immediately adjacent to the level where the circulation department is located.

Stack lighting. In order to facilitate paging and shelving and to make browsing possible, the stacks must be adequately lighted. Wilson and Tauber suggest that 10 to 15 foot-candles is sufficient illumination for finding books quickly and easily.[16] The problem of spreading that light equally over all the shelves can be partially met by tilting the shelves, partially by the use of one of various manufactured shades or globes which tend to focus light on the lower shelves. The use of stack lights should be systematized in each library. The Illinois stack manual sets up

---

[16]Louis Round Wilson and Maurice F. Tauber, The University Library; Its Organization, Administration, and Functions. Chicago: University of Chicago Press, 1945, p.484.

definite directions: aisle and stairwell lights are to be left on all day, as are ranges with light switches on only one end; lights in ranges which have switches at both ends are always to be turned off when not in use.[17] Outlets may be needed for special lamps, microfilm readers, and book cleaning equipment.

Air conditioning the stack. In addition to extremes of temperature and humidity, dust and dirt should be guarded against in the stacks. An air conditioned stack can be the answer to all these problems. It may control the temperature, the humidity, and the amount of dust and bacterial matter present in the air. In general, the condition most desirable for the preservation of books, especially their bindings, coincides with those most desirable for the comfort and health of individuals. The optimum range of temperature for libraries is considered to be 65° F. to 70° F.; the optimum range of humidity 38 to 50 per cent.[18] Further, damage to books is caused not so much by the specific nature of the surrounding air as by variation between extremes of dry and moist conditions.

Temperature and relative humidity. The Bureau of Standards conducted studies to determine under what conditions books could best be preserved. At 65° F., and with a relative humidity of 60 per cent, changes in paper were found to be slight. For human comfort, the winter temperature usually suggested is 70° F., with the corresponding relative humidity from 20 to 50 per cent. During the summer the temperature range should be somewhat higher, from 76° F. to 82° F., with a relative humidity of from 40 to 70 per cent.[19]

Use of carrels. Most large bookstacks have carrels for individual study. Readers with carrel permits usually have the privilege of browsing in the stack where they may take from the shelves the books they wish to use. Sometimes the stack privilege is restricted to certain floors. Books may be taken to a carrel by the reader. If the books are to be used for any appreciable length of time, a special

[17]Ray C. Janeway, University of Illinois Library Stack Manual. Urbana: 1943. (Mimeographed).

[18]R. H. Gates, "Modern Air Treatment," in Herman H. Fussler (ed.), op. cit., p. 115.

[19]Wilson and Tauber, op. cit., p.484-85.

charge form is filled in and placed in each volume. A shelf worker is usually assigned the duty of checking each day the volumes left in the carrels. The page may fill in the data on the cards already inserted, or the carrel user may be expected to fill out the cards for the books. If the latter is true, the page should check the carrel charges for errors or missing information.

Book charging system for carrels. The typical carrel charge card is about 15 inches long, the top 5 inches of which constitutes a "book card" or "charge card" which will interfile with the other circulation charges when it is torn off along its perforated base. The long card remains in the book on the carrel shelf. After tearing off these top cards, the page should take them to the circulation desk, where they will become a part of the central record of books not in their regularly assigned places on the shelves. When the carrel holder finishes using a book, he reverses the form left in the book so that the end marked "return to stacks" or "discharge" projects from the top of the book. The page collects these volumes during the regular inspection each day and clears the charges at circulation.

Directions in the stack. Direction signs, range and shelf labels, and signs indicating any irregularities in shelving should be generously provided throughout the stacks to assist pages, shelvers, and readers who go directly to the stacks in finding proper locations quickly. With modern lettering equipment and some instruction, a page can be trained to do satisfactory work. This is a type of work for which part-time help can be used to advantage, and when employing assistants it would be well to include one or two with lettering ability or training in mechanical drawing. Lettering can be done by using one of the mechanical or controlled lettering sets, which usually contain templates of chosen sizes, a scriber, and a pen. Stencils of thin wood or metal may also be used satisfactorily although there is danger that the stencil may smear the ink.

Chapter 5

CARE OF BOOKS

For the average shelf worker care of books is largely a
matter of proper handling, but shelf workers are partly responsible for the care of the collection and therefore should
have some knowledge of the enemies of books. Enemies
are not always readily recognizable, and danger may lurk
where it is least suspected:

> Sunshine helps free our books from various ene-
> mies, but sunshine will soon deaden many modern
> papers and fade many modern colors in cloth or leather.
> Darkness protects from harmful effects of direct light,
> but darkness encourages molds and insect pests. With
> books or children or most other things the old Greek
> advice against "nothing too much" is as sound today as
> when first uttered....[1]

Proper methods of shelving books

Books should be shelved so that wear or damage will be
at a minimum. Proper handling and shelving will effect
real economies, since carefully handled books last longer,
thus reducing the necessity for early repair, binding, and
replacement. Books being returned to the shelves should
be given special consideration. In the effort to maintain
continuous shelving of discharged volumes books are
often thoughtlessly mistreated. As books are placed on
book trucks, undue crowding should be avoided, since this
loosens the binding.

Books must sometimes be shelved on their fore edges
temporarily, subject to revision before being placed

[1]Harry M. Lydenberg and John Archer, The Care and Repair of Books. 3rd
ed.; New York: R. R. Bowker Co., 1945, p.6.

upright. They should not be left long in this position, for books resting on their fore edges suffer considerable damage. Books should not be placed on top of those already on a book truck unless all of them are piled flat. Even when they are in flat piles, they should not be stacked higher than the top of the ends of the truck, or some of them will probably slip and be damaged by the fall.

Books on the shelves should be arranged so that new acquisitions as well as volumes in circulation can be put in their proper places with little or no shifting. (Do not confuse "shifting" with "straightening," which should be a continuous process.) On a full shelf the books provide their own support. On shelves where there is additional space, book supports should be used to hold the volumes upright. If a shelf is literally filled to capacity, there is danger of damaging all the books on the shelf by attempting to squeeze one more volume into place. Many books have fragile or worn bindings which are damaged by such a procedure. The force required to take a book from a packed shelf will often result in ripping loose the top of the spine covering, the most vulnerable part of a book.

Books on partly filled shelves should occupy the left side of the shelf with the book support bracing them from the right. Paper bound volumes, pamphlets, and current issues of periodicals can suffer severe damage if they are kept upright and not adequately supported. If there is enough space on the shelf, current numbers of most large-size periodicals should lie flat, filed at the ends of their respective runs of bound volumes.

Book supports can be bought from any dealer in library supplies, or any man handy with tools can make them. You need nothing more than an upright held in position firmly enough to assure an upright position to the books next it. Commercial supports are frequently stamped out of a piece of metal cut in the centre and bent to form an upright section. Some have a flange and others not; the former are preferable, since the flange helps prevent the damage done when books are inadvertently pushed against the support as they are put on the shelf. Those with a hook protruding through the bottom of the shelf must be guarded against to make certain they do not harm tall books shelved below.... The homemade varieties suffer in competition with the commercial supports in bulkiness and waste of space.....[2]

Supports with a felt or rubber base to prevent slipping can be purchased. Composition rubber has been used as a base and found to be somewhat unsatisfactory because of its faulty design and its lack of durability.[3] With continued use the bases may become brittle and smooth surfaced. Another kind of support has a hook which protrudes through the bottom of the shelf and may be used with strip or grill type shelving. Still another type of support is made of wire and fits into the flanges on the underside of a shelf, extending downward to hold books in place on the shelf beneath. The standard metal and wire book supports, if without flanges, can easily be adapted for more effective service by making a right angle outward bend in the upright of the metal support or at the bottom of the wire support.[4]

Combatting dirt and dust

For many libraries cleaning is still a tedious job of attempting to combat deposits of dust, dirt, and soot. This is true despite the increasing use of air conditioning in the stacks. Some libraries carry on a constant program of dusting; others clean only periodically. In the smaller libraries the work may be done by the librarians or by the janitor. In university libraries the work is usually done by a special book cleaner, and janitor duty applies more specifically to care of the library building. There is little variation in the equipment used in the cleaning process. A dust cloth, a lamb's wool duster, or a hand brush are standard items in most libraries. The dust cloth, if sprinkled lightly with oil, not only removes the dust but prevents its being spread to resettle upon books already cleaned. A vacuum cleaner of the tank type is an efficient dust remover. A circular brush attachment of standard make,

[2]Ibid., p.13-14.
[3]Bernard B. Lane, "How Do You Shelve?" Wilson Library Bulletin, XV (1941), 643.
[4]Thomas S. Dabagh, "Improved Book Supports," Library Journal, LIII (1928), 260.

about 2-1/2 inches in diameter, is satisfactory. The vacuum should be equipped with a long extension cord and placed on casters so that it can be moved about readily.

Cleaning on a project basis was done at Stephens College. The cleaning squad worked in pairs, each being given a different colored set of fifty cards cut from colored construction paper. The cards were numbered consecutively 1 to 50 in four places, top, bottom, front and back, so that no matter which side was up the number always showed. Use of fifty numbers was based on the fact that no shelf in the library held more than fifty volumes. With different stacks assigned each team, one member would insert the cards in the books as they were taken from the shelf, then pass the books on to his partner who dusted them and stacked them nearby. When the shelf had been scrubbed, the books were returned in their proper sequence of 1, 2, 3, etc., and right side up in order to prevent crushing the cards. Each team then checked the numeral sequence before pulling the cards and moving to the next shelf. This system required more time than had formerly been used, but was considered desirable because it reduced the possibility of misshelving the books.[5]

The full-time book cleaner in a large library follows an easily observed routine. With his equipment, which may be a book truck, dust cloths, and a vacuum cleaner, he removes the books from the shelf in reverse order from right to left and places them on the book truck in the same manner, so that the class numbers read from left to right in their regular order. Once the shelf is thoroughly cleaned with the vacuum, or is wiped clean with a damp cloth, replacing the books is an easy matter. Beginning at the left side of the truck, the worker removes the books and cleans their bindings and paper edges carefully before replacing them on the shelf. If there is danger that a small paper bound volume or pamphlet may be injured by suction, he cleans it with a dust cloth instead of the vacuum.

Bindings are often soiled by ordinary handling and use. Damage to the book can be reduced by applying book varnish or book lacquer which will make the covers sufficiently waterproof to be cleaned with a damp cloth without affecting

[5]Elvajean Hall, "Housecleaning Time Is Here!" Wilson Library Bulletin, XX (1946), 610-11.

the binding. Some libraries use cellophane covers on new books, especially those with attractive jackets. Children's books are often covered. Cellophane covers are considered by many to be satisfactory, since they not only protect the books, but accentuate the colors on jackets and bindings and preserve the biographical data on the book jackets. Rental libraries are using cellophane covers more and more. The Circulation Department of the New York Public Library, using "assembly-line" tactics, processes over 200,000 new books a year with protective jackets.[6]

Maintenance of the collection

Book marking or lettering, though a preparatory process, is an important factor in effective stack management, and some libraries have placed marking (and some mending) in the shelving department. Book numbers must be large enough and distinct enough to be read at a glance. For this purpose a call number of two lines need not be more than 2 centimeters in height. Even with continual use, the book number should remain clear. This may be accomplished by shellacking over the call number. The call numbers should be similar in shape, size, and position on the spines of the books, and spacing should be systematic and even.[7] Re-marking faded call numbers is also necessary for maintaining careful and rapid shelving of books.

Books should be mended when damage first occurs. Inexperienced workers may try to do more mending than is wise, since too much mending tape, and even too much paste, can permanently damage books that are otherwise worth rebinding. Since the pages and shelvers are those who handle the volumes being taken from and sent to the stacks, part of the responsibility for noting the condition of the books properly falls to them. Any book that needs repair should be called to the attention of the stack supervisor or the circulation chief, according to the organization within a particular library.

[6]"New York Public Library Mechanizes Its Processing," Library Journal, LXXV (1950), 188.

[7]Toledo Public Library, Catalog Department, "How to Mark Books," Wilson Library Bulletin, XV (1941), 768-69.

In order to keep books in proper sequence, shelves must be read constantly, especially where readers are permitted to browse at will. Shelf reading is a continuous process and is usually among the duties assigned to trained, nonprofessional staff members. Shelf reading can be done more systematically by requiring each assistant to keep a daily record of his work. Books in open shelf rooms may be the responsibility of the librarian immediately in charge of that room. In such a situation, assistance in reading shelves may be provided from some other source. In the bookstack, reading shelves is usually done by pages who are scheduled for this duty during slack hours. Some librarians, because of service demands and lack of sufficient help, find it possible to provide for adequate shelf reading only in the few days between terms or at the end of the regular school year. At those times, circulation staff members as well as pages and shelvers are assigned to read certain sections of the stacks as rapidly as their other duties permit. While classes are in session, general shelf reading may be confined to spot checking, reading in those areas reported to be in disorder, and continuous reading of the most used sections.

Preservation of bindings

Librarians who wish to go thoroughly into the question of the care of books should take advantage of Lydenberg and Archer's careful study of that subject.[8] Only the three most frequently occurring problems will be treated, quite briefly, here: mildew, vermin, and preservation of leather bindings.

Mildew can best be combatted by prevention - proper air, light, and relative humidity conditions. Use pans of dry calcium chloride to pull the moisture out of the air if there is too much dampness, especially in basement storage.

There are two types of dessicants in common use...: adsorbers which condense water vapor on their inner surfaces, but can be reactivated, and absorbers which change chemically or physically as they absorb water.

[8]Lydenberg and Archer, op. cit.

Silica gel and activated alumina are examples of the
first type. Dry calcium chloride is the most widely
used of the second type, although solutions of lithium
chloride, calcium chloride and others are sometimes
employed.[9]

Use a hygrometer to measure relative humidity and do not
worry too much about dampness until the relative humidity
reaches 65 and tends to stay there. (Remember that ex-
treme, continued dryness is just as harmful, and guard
against a relative humidity that continues to be under 38.)
Mildew inhibitors are sold by library and bindery supply
houses. They come in liquid form, at reasonable prices,
and are accompanied by specific directions for their use.

Vermin can be controlled best by proper housing of the
collection, adequate light and ventilation, and again, proper
attention to relative humidity. Silverfish poisons are made
and marketed by chemical companies, and should be used
where these pests have become destructive.

Preservation of leather bindings can be accomplished
to a large degree by "...vaseline, varnish, air, sun,
strength, patience, observation and time."[10] Some prefer
a lanolin and oil dressing to the vaseline.[11] The limited
effectiveness of these external preparations should, however, be recognized:

Of the various leather finishes examined by Mr.
Innes a certain shellac preparation was found to be
most effective in this respect and cellulose was high on
the list; and both are in a measure protective as long
as the film does not crack, but it would be very difficult
to prevent this along the hinges. Aqueous preparations
of oils and greases, however, were found to be almost
entirely non-effective, and as most dressings come
within this category they cannot claim to afford any
protection in the sense of arresting chemical decay.
The main claim for leather dressings is that they "feed"
the skin, acting as a lubricant for the fibrous tissue,

[9]"Dehumidifying--the Remedy for Mildew, Dampness and the Discomfort
Caused by High Humidities," Architectural Forum, LXXXI (August, 1944), 12.

[10]G. E. Wire, "Leather Preservation," Library Journal, LIII (1928), 586.

[11]Lydenberg and Archer, op. cit., p.83-84.

preventing it from drying up and cracking. Let us examine this claim a little more closely.

Those having the care of books are accustomed to refer to the powdery decay as a "drying up" whereas leather in such a condition can be shown by analysis to contain its usual quota of water. The phenomenon is one that no grease can prevent. The lubricating effect is entirely unrelated to powdery disintegration. Such things as Turkey Red Oil, Castor or Neats' Foot Oil make leather "supple," a desirable quality in moving parts of saddlery, belting, etc., and occasional treatment with a little good dressing of suitable quality cannot harm the hinges of a book and will be advantageous. But the treatment thus given is for the lesser evil only, namely wear and tear.[12]

[12]H. J. Plenderleith, The Preservation of Leather Bookbindings. London: British Museum, 1946, p.18-19.

Chapter 6

THE SHELF LIST AND INVENTORY

The shelf list

Definition and uses. Miss Mann defines the shelf list as:

> a catalog of books in the order in which they stand on the shelves. Each title is represented by a card giving the author, title, edition, number of volumes (if more than one), number of copies (if more than one), call number and other items as the library deems necessary. The call number determines the arrangement of the cards in the shelf list in the same way as it has already determined the arrangement of the books on the shelves.[1]

The shelf list is the most useful of the library records for shelf workers although they are not responsible for it. It is used to establish entry or to get further information concerning copies, location, etc., either (1) when the call number only is known or (2) when other information is incomplete or needs verification. The shelf list is also the indispensable tool in taking inventory since it is arranged in the order in which books stand on the shelves.

Most libraries use the standard shelf list as defined by Miss Mann. Some use an accession book, some sheet shelf lists for continuations while others employ other ingenious and sometimes quite satisfactory devices as substitutes for the standard shelf list.

Availability. In some libraries the shelf list is looked upon as the property of the catalog department, and use by

---

[1]Margaret Mann, Introduction to Cataloging and the Classification of Books. 2d. ed.; Chicago: American Library Association, 1943, p.94.

pages and the public is discouraged. The reason often given for this is that the shelf list must be maintained as a dependable record by call number of the holdings of the library and there is great danger that cards will be withdrawn, misfiled, or disturbed in some other way. This reason is supported by the facts that shelf list cards often do not have holes punched in them, drawers in the cabinets are often not equipped with rods, or the rods are not used on the basis that cards go in and out of the shelf list so often that rods are impractical. All this reasoning is perfectly logical, if one accepts the premise that the shelf list is the sole property of the catalog department. At the University of Illinois a duplicate shelf list is kept in a public area and has become an important adjunct to the dictionary catalog, for the shelf list is a kind of classified catalog. Where the shelf list has been made accessible to the public and its use explained and encouraged it has been found to be extremely valuable. To restrict its use to staff only (and sometimes only a part of the staff) is to refute the basic concept of a library as a service agency which should be run for the reader, not for the staff. If the trays need rods, then the answer is to get rods in the trays or to get trays with rods, as the case may be, but certainly not to restrict the use of the shelf list. This restricted use is a very common practice even though discovery of the shelf list has proved to be a delight to the reader, especially the subject specialist.

A time-saver in paging. As far as the shelf worker is concerned, particularly the page, he simply must be given access to the shelf list if he is to do efficient work rapidly. Tests made at Brown University, plus observance and study of the problem in other libraries, lead to the conclusion that the speed and accuracy of a nonprofessional library worker, such as a page, is appreciably increased when he is allowed to check his call slip against the shelf list rather than in the public catalog. Lessons learned in shelving and paging can be applied to locating a card in the shelf list, but the dictionary catalog, particularly in a large library, is an extremely complicated thing and difficult for a page to use without considerable instruction.

Inventory

Responsibility for inventory. In some libraries inventory is done by the catalog department, in others by the circulation department. Still other systems have most of the work done by circulation but under the supervision of the catalog department. In some public library systems inventory is the responsibility of the catalog department which depends upon circulation for much of the routine work in the main library building and upon each branch librarian, with help from the catalog department, for inventory in the branches. In still other systems inventory is a joint responsibility, usually of the catalog and circulation departments. Under all these systems, the preliminary steps in taking inventory are essentially shelf work. Only the catalog department can resolve many of the problems raised by inventory, for example, duplication of call numbers, questions involving location and copy number, discrepancies between call number and book number whether they appear on the books, in the books, on the shelf list or in the catalog. The practice of placing the responsibility for inventory taking with the catalog department in the large library is sometimes questioned, but is recommended. Wilson and Tauber have well stated the case for this practice:

> Generally, the responsibility for taking inventory is delegated to the catalog department. Sometimes it is shared with the circulation department. Inventories may be continual or may be made at stated intervals.
>
> Inventories usually reveal situations which affect the catalog department and other members of the staff. The administrator must make decisions concerning the withdrawal of cards for books which are missing, stolen, or discarded; suggest replacements with the cooperation of circulation and departmental librarians; and select items for rebinding. Inventories may reveal inconsistencies in cataloging and classification which require correction. [2]

[2]Louis Round Wilson and Maurice F. Tauber, The University Library; Its Organization, Administration, and Functions. Chicago: University of Chicago Press, 1945, p.172-73.

General procedure. For most types of libraries Mr. Trotier's concise outline of inventory procedure has general applicability:

> The taking of inventory involves the checking, with the shelf list, of the book collection and of records which account for the whereabouts of books not located on the shelves. Its chief purpose is to discover what books are missing from the library and unaccounted for so that those which are not found may be either replaced or withdrawn from the catalog records. The detection of discrepancies in library records and the discovery of books in need of repair are incidental but useful by-products of the process.
>
> The general procedure for taking inventory includes the following steps: (1) arranging the books in correct order on the shelves; (2) comparing the shelf-list cards in their order with the corresponding books on the shelves and noting any books not found there; (3) checking the record of books not located with the circulation records and other records which might account for these books; (4) making a periodic search for missing books; (5) replacing lost books which are needed by the library; and (6) canceling or withdrawing catalog records of books not found or replaced.[3]

Of the six steps just enumerated, shelf workers are responsible for number 1 and number 4, share responsibility for number 2, and sometimes assist in number 3.

Frequency of inventory. Not all libraries take inventory every year. As a matter of fact, some libraries have ceased taking inventory altogether. The decision as to whether inventory should or should not be taken may not always rest with the library administrator. It may be that the responsibilities of his office formally or tacitly require that an inventory be taken. This problem will have to be resolved in each library situation but for most libraries, whether or not inventory is considered administratively mandatory, a thorough check-up on the book collection is

---

[3]Arnold H. Trotier, "Cataloging and Classification," in Guy R. Lyle, The Administration of the College Library. 2d. ed.; New York: H. W. Wilson Co., 1949, p.117-18.

needed at regular intervals in order to maintain desirable standards of service. Because of variation in library situations and needs, recommendations regarding frequency of inventory are not attempted here. Libraries should consider annual, biennial, triennial, or departmental inventories as will fit their size and organization.

A general trend away from complete annual inventories was in progress over twenty years ago, and substitutes were being discussed.[4] Among the substitutes is the "book census," which consists of a count of the books in each class that are on the shelves and can be accounted for by circulation and other records. The number of books arrived at in this manner is subtracted from the accession records, thus revealing the number of books missing. The book census does not, of course, show what books are missing and therefore would not satisfy all inventory needs. A relatively old description of a book census involving a count of almost half a million books but requiring only about four hours' time might still be of interest to librarians considering this method.[5]

Continuous inventory vs. project inventory. Continuous inventory, a self-explanatory phrase, is employed in some libraries, and is especially popular with the very large public or research library systems where it would be impossible to take inventory in a limited space of time even if the whole staff were utilized. Continuous inventory is also more desirable than project inventory (taking complete inventory at one time) in the very large system because the problems arising out of inventory are fed steadily into the catalog and order departments. This is better than flooding those departments periodically with great batches of snags which would tend to disrupt normal activity. Some school and college libraries have periods when school is closed, during which time records are not constantly in use, the staff is not very busy with regular duties, and, with the faculty absent, order and cataloging have slowed down. It may even be possible to close the college library while taking inventory.

Procedure for a small library. Here are a number of

---

[4]"Frequency of Inventory," Library Journal, LII (1927), 827-28.
[5]Arthur E. Bostwick, "A New Kind of Inventory," Library Journal, XLII (1917), 369-71.

suggestions regarding inventory taking in a school library which might prove helpful to the inexperienced librarian in a small library:

An inventory must be taken every year in most school libraries. Procedure is much the same as elsewhere, that is, books on the shelves and in circulation are checked against the shelf list and losses counted. The inventory can very well be turned over to a clerical assistant who may be aided by pupil checkers. In one school, inventory is taken by the clerical assistant during the spring recess. It can be carried on piecemeal during the year. It is unfortunate, and usually unnecessary, to close the library.

Having ascertained through inventory that certain books are missing or must be discarded, it might be supposed that notations to that effect should be entered at once on shelf-list and accession records. But books missing from school library shelves have a way of turning up unexpectedly. The annual summer cleaning of the building invariably brings to light library treasures buried under the rubbish in lockers or reposing behind radiators. Other books annoyingly absent from the shelves one month are present the next. Altogether, it is wise to place a temporary signal on the shelf-list card and then wait a while before marking the item "Missing" or "Lost" in traditional red ink.[6]

Procedure for a university library. Miss Fargo's suggested procedure is detailed enough to serve as an inventory-taking guide for most small libraries. The larger library will follow a more complex process. The following inventory procedure is the one used at the University of Tennessee:

The catalog department and the circulation department take the inventory under the supervision of the head of the catalog department. The stacks are read in preparation for inventory by personnel furnished from all departments. The reading is so scheduled as to use staff members who can be spared from regular duties for periods of one hour

---

[6]Lucile F. Fargo, The Library in the School. 4th ed.; Chicago: American Library Association, 1947, p. 271-72.

twice a day. It is begun where the inventory is to start and is completed as quickly as possible so that misshelved books are correctly shelved. All discharged books in a section scheduled to be inventoried on a particular day are shelved immediately.

The inventory process uses teams of two staff members, one from the catalog department and one from the circulation department. A team works no longer than two hours at a time, for mistakes due to fatigue seem to increase after about two hours of such detailed work. More than one team works at a time if the follow-up work of typing charges and making corrections keeps apace.

The catalog department member of the team must be one who can interpret the shelf list readily and make necessary notes regarding corrections. The records used are the shelf list and the charge cards from the circulation department for the section to be checked. A book truck of convenient height is used by the cataloger as a work table. The top shelf holds the shelf-list and charge-card trays. The lower shelf is used for items removed from the stack shelves for any reason, such as re-marking, mending, binding, or correction in call number. The cataloging assistant reads a call number and the circulation assistant checks the shelf and indicates to the cataloger whether the book is in place. Items checked are copies, numbers, volumes, etc., as listed on the shelf card. When a book is missing the cataloger checks the charge file and, if there is no card for it, puts a clip on the shelf card. If merely a copy or issue is missing, she clips a slip of paper noting this to the shelf card.

Unbound, complete volumes of periodicals are removed from the shelf to be bound, and recorded on a slip which is then clipped to the shelf card. No notation is made of material removed from the shelf for re-marking, since these corrections are made immediately. If there is material on the shelf that is not in the shelf list, a notation is clipped to the shelf card, or the material is removed from the shelf for correction by the catalog department. As the checking of each shelf-list tray is completed, a member of the cir- . culation department types charge cards for all missing material and material sent for binding. The cataloging staff then makes changes and corrections as indicated by clips and notes on the shelf-list cards. The charge cards

for missing material are stamped "missing inventory."
The "missing inventory" cards are checked with the shelf
list and catalog. A search is made for the missing books
in the reading rooms, stacks, etc., before the charge cards
are filed in the general circulation file. When inventory is
completed these cards are pulled and rechecked, and decisions made regarding replacements and withdrawals.

Chapter 7

PERSONNEL MANAGEMENT

The perennial question of part-time help

One of the most important personnel problems faced in any library is the use of part-time help as opposed to full-time help. While this question can be answered only by the administrative staff of each library, one helpful generalization is: Part-time help should be used to supplement full-time help rather than to replace it. Full-time help should be used wherever possible up to the point of great variation in work load; part-time help should be used to meet the need for additional help at a given time where the load is not constantly at a high level. The college librarian will, of course, immediately think of the desirability of using student assistants primarily or even entirely for paging and shelving books. The advantages of using student assistants include interesting the college student in library work as a career, giving employment to the student who may need a job, and using pages who have had some college training. All of these reasons, however, are hardly sufficient to weight the decision in favor of entire dependence upon part-time help when the primary function of the library--good service--may suffer materially.

It has always seemed a bit ironical that this important aspect of library service--shelf work--should be supposed, somehow or other, to be done well by miscellaneous student-assistant or other part-time help when, in the same library, other work of no more importance is stubbornly argued as being impossible to accomplish under such training and scheduling hazards. The suggested dividing line between full-time and part-time help still allows for considerable part-time help. Changeover to a use of full-time shelf workers usually results in a recognizable improvement in service. The notion that all pages must be student assistants is so firmly entrenched in the minds of so many people that in the literature of the subject the words are generally used synonymously. This is indeed an unfortunate fixation. In meeting most library problems, full consideration is usually given to personnel matters. To limit the field of possible personnel recruitment to a group of students who by definition and in most cases by college regulation are restricted to part-time service is to encumber unnecessarily the solution of the problem under consideration. With such a handicap high standards will be difficult to attain.

Part-time help in school libraries is a special consideration since student assistants do the shelving as part of their school service and as part of their education in the organization and use of libraries. The duty of shelving is rotated along with other duties, even though more speed and efficiency would result from specialization. With the large amount of student and supervisory time devoted to this duty in the larger school libraries, paid student or clerical help regularly responsible for shelving might be cheaper and more efficient in the long run.

Recruiting for shelf work

A formal tabulation of the personality and character requirements for shelf work personnel would read very much like those for anything else, probably beginning with such essentials as honesty, initiative, dependability, and ending with a list of more specific habits and skills such as accuracy, neatness, and eagerness to learn. Such a formal tabulation will not be attempted here in the effort to set forth some realistic and measurable factors which may be found useful in trying to assemble a group of people who will be able to do a reasonably good job of shelf work in the average library.

The first thing to do in determining what personnel is required is to break down the positions into as many full-time jobs as would seem to approximate the full-time load. Only in the very small library would this result in no full-time staff at all. A study of variations in load by day, hour, season, etc., will give an idea of the part-time jobs to be filled. The next logical step is to find out what kind of help is available. Then, by working between these two stabilized "knowns" the usual compromises between what is wanted and what is available can be made, and the next step--seeing what help can actually be obtained--begun.

A good source from which to obtain these workers is often the placement officers in the local high schools. If the library will make a report to the school on each assistant who is employed by the library as a page, the high school placement officer will realize that filling a page position in a college or university library is often tantamount to sending the better student on to college. The library administration should consider it a responsibility to see that a good page does not get "stuck" on the job for more than two years. In times of intense labor shortages the high school graduate and his placement officer may feel quite properly that too great a sacrifice is made by working at a page position for a year or two before going back to school.

There is no really effective system of personnel recruitment for shelf workers in times of labor shortages, but the one which most people depend upon is to use girls instead of boys. Some libraries prefer girls for pages at all times, and they do appear to be neater and more accurate workers than boys. One public librarian with considerable experience with shelf workers insists that girls are also more dependable, especially in regard to coming to work, for the boys are "forever getting off to play ball!" On the other hand, some phases of shelf work are rather strenuous (such as paging bound newspapers, heavy periodicals, etc., and shifting books), and this fact constitutes an objection to the use of girl pages.

The new shelf worker

When a new shelf worker first reports for duty, the personnel officer, the librarian, the shelf work supervisor, or whoever is the logical person in the particular system, should explain to him immediately the following: (1) the person to whom he will be officially responsible; (2) the organizational place of shelf work in the particular system, the importance of shelf work, and how it affects library service; (3) general regulations affecting all employees or employees of his classification; (4) the potentialities of the position, that is, salary increases (whether on length of

63

service or solely on a merit basis), opportunity for advancement within the department or library if he continues as a shelf worker, opportunities for advancement within the library in positions other than shelf work (such as photographic laboratories, nonprofessional circulation work, bindery, etc.); (5) exactly what the salary is, when and how often he will be paid, as well as how check or cash payroll is handled. By all means it should be pointed out at this time what deductions will be made for federal income tax and, depending upon the institution, whether or not there will be any other deductions for health insurance, retirement, social security, etc. If possible, he should not be asked too early to make a decision regarding options affecting his pay, since too often these take the form of impositions in the mind of the worker.

The training he is to receive as far as shelf work is concerned should certainly be received under the person responsible for shelf work. This training varies, but the following constitutes a minimum: (1) He should be introduced briefly to the idea of and the necessity for classification of books, with principal stress, of course, on the part that has to deal with the classification number being a "call" or "shelf" number. (2) He should be given instructions in what might be called "shelf-list" order, based on the classification used, including author numbers, volume numbers, etc. Some libraries have successfully used a set of cards for practice work, with the supervisor correcting mistakes and explaining the principle involved in each instance. Other librarians have, with apparently equal success, used a group of books as a practice set, much in the same manner as the practice set of cards. (3) He should then shelve under supervision. (4) The next step is to have him shelve independently but subject to revision. This can be accomplished by having him place all the books on their fore edges with about one third of the book protruding, so that his reviser can readily detect the volumes to be checked and put them in an erect position if they are correctly shelved.

Paging books is much easier than shelving them because there is so much more uncertainty involved in the latter process. For example, when a page finds the book matching his call slip he knows he has found the right place on the shelf, but the inexperienced shelver is not sure that

64 Personnel management

where he thinks a book belongs is its proper location. Further, if there is an apparent choice between two locations, he is unable to make a decision whereas the page can look in both places if he does not find the book in the first one searched. Because shelving is more difficult it is better to start shelf workers with shelving and its demanding exactness rather than with paging. The opposite is usually done because paging is actually so simple in relation to shelving that often a new page can start to work in the morning and be doing a fair job of paging before the end of the day. It takes much longer to develop a good shelver.

Some libraries have found it desirable to have a set of "rules of conduct." One used at the University of Illinois, which is designed for stack personnel, reads in part as follows:

1. Give assistance to any library patron who may approach you in the stacks. 2. Only necessary conversation should be carried on and that in the quietest possible manner. Avoid all other. 3. Be prompt to report to work. If it is necessary to be absent report the need to the Stack Supervisor as early as possible. 4. Do your share, be considerate of your fellow workers. 5. Service should be the keynote of all action while on duty.[1]

Such a set of regulations should prove helpful in any library.

It is usually best to stress accuracy at the beginning of a new shelf worker's training and then gradually work toward speed without sacrificing accuracy. Studies have shown that in shelf work, as in so many other types of activity, speed does not necessarily mean that accuracy need be sacrificed. As a matter of fact, often the fast worker is the most accurate.[2]

Interviews with stack supervisors and first-hand observations prove that one generalization on training shelf work personnel can be made: The page's attitude toward his work

---

[1]Ray C. Janeway, University of Illinois Library Stack Manual. Urbana : 1943. (Mimeographed).

[2]Nancy S. Loehr, "Studies Shelving Speed," Library Journal, LXXI (1946), 1191-92.

is a very important factor. This fact should never be forgotten by either the supervisor or the shelf worker.

Personnel management routines

If there is enough shelf work to justify a full-time shelf work supervisor, his headquarters should usually be set up in the stack itself. This makes supervision much easier and allows the shelf workers ready access to their supervisor for the many problems that arise in connection with shelving, paging, shifting, and general housekeeping in the stacks. A simple arrangement used with success is to utilize a carrel for the stack supervisor's "office."

The shelf work supervisor keeps the personnel records for time schedules and substitutions. In small libraries a clerical assistant in circulation may be assigned this work. Systematic and orderly payroll routines are of greatest importance. A shelf worker, as anyone else, wants to be confident that anything in any way affecting his pay is being flawlessly handled. He should not have to track someone down in order to report the hours worked. He should not have to find it necessary to wander about looking for someone else who is wandering about, in order to get his pay check or voucher. He should not have to worry about mistakes in records of time worked, overtime, time off, and in payroll. If he is to be impressed with the desirability of accuracy, it is well not to make mistakes in the records affecting him.

The assignment of assistants according to time and place is the principal purpose of scheduling. A careful study of circulation peaks is the only way to determine the number of pages which should be on duty at a given time. It should be remembered that periods of peak loads are the places where part-time assistants for pages will be found most useful. Local studies showing what classes of books are called for most frequently help to determine (1) the relative location of the books in the stacks in the first place and (2) the number of pages to assign to a particular stack level, reading room or area, depending upon the physical layout of the library. Schedules should be posted so that everyone will know who is on duty, where he is, and what type of work he is supposed to be doing. It should be assumed that schedules hold until specific and formal exception has been made. All substituting should be approved by the stack supervisor or his administrative equivalent well in advance of the actual hour of reporting for work. While getting the work done must be given precedence, schedules should nevertheless be as reasonable and humane as possible. No one should be assigned to reading shelves all day, every day, indefinitely; no one should be assigned to work more than two evenings a week unless he actually prefers more than what would ordinarily be considered an equitable share of undesirable hours. Week-end schedules should be evenly divided among all the workers. This point is particularly important, as it seems to be the cause of more dissatisfaction among pages than any other single scheduling inequity. The best solution to these scheduling problems is to recruit with them in mind, employing an adequate number of workers who prefer these particular work periods.

If there are many shelf workers scattered throughout the library system, there should be some formal manner of checking them in. A time clock is perhaps the most dependable. Some stack supervisors prefer to see each assistant as he reports for work in order to give any instructions necessary for the day, since problems arise causing hurried changes in plans. In some cases the stack supervisor likes to have the pages check out with him, reporting progress on shelf reading and shelving and allowing the supervisor and the page to discuss some of the questions that are bound to arise in a conscientious shelf worker's mind. In many ways this is a very good practice, because it does let both the supervisor and the assistant know that they will see each other at the end of the day or work period; it relieves both of the necessity of searching for the other should the question not be one that must be resolved immediately. Many of these questions are relatively minor ones of choice which can be more or less arbitrarily decided, since there is no right or wrong to many of them, but merely a right or wrong in relation to the particular library's practice. However, in shelf work as in cataloging and bibliographical method, consistency is a primary criterion, and in order to be consistent in shelf work it is desirable to have even these minor decisions made by supervisors, not the individual shelf workers.

Rest periods should be scheduled so that service will

not be interrupted. The frequency and length of rest periods will depend upon local conditions. It is unwise to decide upon the length of rest periods first and then try to enforce observance. A more satisfactory procedure is to learn how long a rest period must be to allow time for refreshment and an unhurried chat. If this requires very much time (over fifteen minutes) the rest periods should be less frequent. Some libraries require assistants to make up rest period time, but many libraries do not require that it be made up. The latter practice is recommended. Few experienced supervisors would be inclined to disagree with the following statement regarding rest pauses:

> The results of the present investigation...seem to indicate that both unauthorized rest can be reduced and production can be increased by authorized rest pauses even when the worker is made to pay for his rest by a longer working day. They further indicate that conditions under which the authorized rest is taken must be made as free from sources of irritation as possible if the worker is to accept the policy without undue dissatisfaction. Finally, the results indicate that, in clerical as well as in industrial work, employees secure rest pauses even if they are not specifically granted by the management.[3]

[3]William McGehee and Edwin B. Owen, "Authorized and Unauthorized Rest Pauses in Clerical Work," Journal of Applied Psychology, XXIV (1940), 613.